E E Y H N
V R T I G

(EVERYTHING)

KIMBERLEE ANDERSON

Copyright © 2025 Kimberlee Anderson.

All rights reserved. No part of this book may be reproduced, stored, or transmitted by any means—whether auditory, graphic, mechanical, or electronic—without written permission of both publisher and author, except in the case of brief excerpts used in critical articles and reviews. Unauthorized reproduction of any part of this work is illegal and is punishable by law.

ISBN: 979-8-89419-736-4 (sc)
ISBN: 979-8-89419-737-1 (hc)
ISBN: 979-8-89419-738-8 (e)

Because of the dynamic nature of the Internet, any web addresses or links contained in this book may have changed since publication and may no longer be valid. The views expressed in this work are solely those of the author and do not necessarily reflect the views of the publisher, and the publisher hereby disclaims any responsibility for them.

One Galleria Blvd., Suite 1900, Metairie, LA 70001
(504) 702-6708

CONTENTS

Acknowledgment v
Introduction vii
Chapter 1   The Story Begins 1
Chapter 2   In The Hood 4
Chapter 3   Round and Round 8
Chapter 4   Branch by Branch 12
Chapter 5   I Am 16
Chapter 6   Knowledge is Power 21
Chapter 7   Meant To Be 25
Chapter 8   Suddenly 28
Chapter 9   Let There Be Light 32
Chapter 10 The Battle 35
Chapter 11 Good Vibes Only 39
Chapter 12 One Small Mustard Seed 43
Chapter 13 10 x Fold 47
Chapter 14 Loose Strings 51
Chapter 15 The Reunion 57
Chapter 16 Truth Be Told 62
Chapter 17 Libra Scales 70
Chapter 18 Now You See Me, Now You Don't 74
Chapter 19 The Golden Era 84
Chapter 20 Elohim's Proof 88
Conclusion 93

ACKNOWLEDGMENT

THE EASY QUR'AN

Translation of the **HOLY QUR'AN** in Easy English with explanatory notes and reasons of revelation.

By

Imtiaz Ahmad

A True Story Written Testimonial

Told By

Kimberlee Anderson
January 29, 2024

INTRODUCTION

Welcome, Readers.

Have you read a good book lately?

I laugh at this question myself as reading had never been a hobby of preoccupation, but never say never! We should routinely try doing something different inevitably, or teachings that one could learn may signify limitations, concurrent to surpass. Guidance and Knowledge push a weaker individual into a stronger, magnetic, outspoken living entity. The circle of life in this society is we're BORN on Earth, we GROW, we LEARN while living, and then there's DEATH.

Is that really it?

Every day comes along bearing a different task, motive, or troublesome disturbance that we as people must conquer. I have learned in my evolution of time, that wisdom is infiltrated and the mind is more important or fragile than one may think. Be careful.

What if you found out **patience** is a virtue and **invincibility** is timeless?

The naked eye can only see so much, but yet be a target for observations of progression by you and me, indefinitely. As you read, open your mind to the endless possibilities because what you are about to witness are actually based on **my** true events. In this day and age like many centuries ago, there was and has been a distinction between the GOOD, the BAD, and the EVIL that roam spontaneously throughout planet Earth.

First, let's begin with **"He"** who beautifully made ALL OF HIS CREATION in six days, then rested and blessed on the seventh.

EVERYTHING

Dedicated
to
GOD

CHAPTER 1

THE STORY BEGINS

They call it "The Boot," Southern Louisiana, home of the New Orleans Saints, and this is where the Miller family resides. Parents, George and Claudia, are married with two children, Jade and Brian, who are three years apart, living in a three-bedroom home. In the River Parishes, everyone knows everyone, but the Miller family kept their business to themselves. George would be stern and straight to the point, while Claudia was passive and nurturing. There wasn't much talking in this household because George got along better with the bottle of Seagram's Gin at the peak of every sunset. Dinner had to be prepared every night during the same time or his temperament of a mad man's abuse came out, physically and emotionally. Claudia tried to stay away from George, by locking herself in other rooms, but he just kicked their doors down, literally off of the hinges. Brian played video games all night and could care less, but Jade wanted the peace more than anything else. She'd rather turn her television volume down instead of the opposite, listening out for times of tumultuous damage, interrupting her mindset. Most nights ended with rapid fistfights, broken items, and holes in walls, as their end resulted meaning for goodnight. Oh yeah, about dinner, that was always cold, but at least something had been left, no complaints. Once George went out finally, no one dared to press the smallest button on the microwave.

E E Y H N V R T I G : (EVERYTHING)

Claudia's weeping and sniffling would always be the background, given with a silent night of whispers. He rose the next morning, ready for work, always steadfast in paying bills on time, not a cent short. Employed as a successful welder, who took his money very seriously, everything they spent had passed through him or it absolutely did not happen. Mrs. Miller headed to her retail job and the kids took their bus to school, completing the normal day. Unfortunately, 2:30 p.m. came for Jade, school brought the only relieving way to exit that house. She dreaded it so bad, that at fifteen years of age, her first job felt like a pleasant vacation away from the distractions of an unwelcoming household. Jade started her search for a part-time gig, in months, she could legally work and be thrilled without reason. The more hours for her the better; Jade didn't care if she had to flip fries, run a register, or mop floors. Being able to buy what she wanted, came right in time for preparations for her senior year. While working she encountered many new people, one of them was a girl named Naomi, who was a coworker that became a friend. They worked the same shift and although different in character, they were able to get along well, which couldn't be figured out by others.

Naomi enjoyed doing her own thing, getting little discipline growing up, and Jade carried a more sheltered life, majority of the time. Since Jade kept the stable job, consecutively for months, George felt it would be safe to get her first car. She graduated high school by completing assignments and holding an average GPA, hoping things at home could get better. One day after work, Jade came home to see her parents in another explosive argument and the close of their door made George more upset. He began cursing at her for the last time; she had never talked back or disrespected her father, but that day carried a different stance. After giving George a piece of her mind and a few choice words, he told Jade to remove herself out of his home at seventeen years old. That was that!

At this point, Jade didn't care where she had to go. Not spending another night in that chaotic household meant relaxation for her. George took back her car so she called another coworker who gave her a ride out for a place to sleep through the night. No longer concerned about the gloominess, Jade had relief just to breathe calmly, without hearing the fighting of family drama anymore. Naomi lived in an apartment complex of one-bedroom studios that recently became vacant for one new tenant. Jade called Gary, the landlord, asking about availability and if he would be willing to rent one out to her, being seventeen years old.

He said Yes!

With having just a twin-sized futon, a refrigerator, and a stove, there had been nothing else Jade needed or could ask for. The emptiness gave her peace. She finally felt like there was no place like home.

    No Curfews

        No Attitudes and

            No Seagram's Gin

CHAPTER 2

IN THE HOOD

As she woke up the next day relaxed, Jade didn't realize freedom came with the struggles of adulthood and finding your own way to get around, carless. George refused to let her see it, let alone use it, so money became her motive, which she did not mind working for. When at work her fellow coworkers would all get along, so working together made it easier to accept transportation, back and forth, from there and home. Jade ended up getting promoted to a shift manager position, but paydays were only twice a month, so rent and her bills took most of it. She started working when three men walked in. As Jade assisted some customers' orders, she felt a stare from someone burning a hole in the back of her head. One of the men could not stop observing her. He bit into his food saying nothing at all, but gave a lasting glimpse of interest for remembrance. After an hour, the business phone rang. She sled to the back to grab it, shocked by the male who asked to speak with Jade Miller. He introduced himself as Tylor or T.C., whichever she had liked, quickly adding that it had been him who left earlier, not able to keep eyes on his food. This man was tall and handsome. Jade couldn't help but be flattered in a strange kind of way, so they exchanged numbers, speaking on the phone for hours every day. Eventually, after hanging together for a while, they officially became a couple, going on a few outings here and there.

T.C. lived somewhat in the fast lane. Being raised by a single mother, he had to grow up doing things in the street that he learned to hide well. He showed up to her spot holding a bag of weed, asking if she wanted to try a little and how they should enjoy his birthday, but Jade had never smoked. Curious to try the natural plant she had always heard of in movies and songs, they sat outside in the moonlit night, enjoying Jade's first experience, of that one time she would not forget. A few more months went by with them progressively seeing each other. They did mash well, but even potatoes go bad after a while. The relationship ended just as fast as it started. T.C. carried that player role, wanting Jade for himself, but still could not be faithful. She decided to do her own thing from then on, hanging with Naomi more often when they weren't working their ten-hour shifts. These two seemed totally different. Naomi's stomping ground were the projects, but it didn't take long for Jade to go from not knowing the area to fitting right in. The buildings had small window units, busted screen doors with broken handles, and graffiti-written brick walls.

Everyone Naomi knew wanted to know who Jade was. She undeniably stood out, having a beautiful melanin complexion pressed against a thick, in-all-the-right-places type of exterior. Any time of the day, they would walk a railroad track that led them into the projects and easily catch a ride back home before dark. When they walked inside Naomi's place, her abusive baby daddy, Shotgun, had been sitting on the sofa, watching their daughter, Toy. Jade could tell he was not all that and a bag of chips. He gave Naomi a look out of this world, causing their guest absolute discomfort to leave. The little girl, Toy, gave her a hug goodbye, and politely went back to play with her dolls on their living room floor, alone. On the following day, right before Jade's work shift, she saw Naomi sitting outside on the steps with an ugly black eye. Jade wanted to make sure she was okay but Naomi just smiled, telling her it couldn't be love if a man didn't hit his woman. They say love is blind, however, she just became blinded, period.

You never knew when Shotgun would appear and leave again, but Jade thinks Naomi started doing the most when she was not getting punched. Every Friday night to enjoy their weekends, the two ladies began going to Kreams for their big cup night. The hottest spot to be was Kreams, a hole in the wall that always stayed jammed pack, with one way in and one way out. Heat or sweat did not stop the dope dealers, entangled with their neighborhood hoes from pulling up, and it damn sure didn't prevent Jade and Naomi from having a great time. Both women were dressed to be seen as they walked to the bar for a few alcoholic beverages. Naomi knew when there would be things or drama going on. She couldn't help being good at keeping her mouth open and not closed, if you know what I mean. As they stood in the corner, a group of club hoppers were staring pretty hard, and a verbal altercation between Naomi and one of them broke out. Jade could only pay attention to fingers and curse words floating in the air, but before the situation became worse, bar security escorted both of them outside.

She didn't realize how careful she needed to be around Naomi; however, this would, soon be shown to her, eventually. The next day, both were chilling outside of Naomi's place, chatting it up, when a car was heard coming down the street toward them. Naomi knew the sounds of every dope dealer's engine, bass, and probably their air conditioner, which made it easier for her to speak of who came, beforehand. Now Jade realized why that one crack stayed in Naomi's blinds. One's noisy tendencies were because her time had been made for it. A brown Cutlass Supreme pulled up with a black male inside. His door swung open as Naomi said, it was someone named Bags.

Bags walked up to them, wearing a gold Cuban link chain, some black and white Jordans, and a loud-smelling blunt. He spoke to Naomi but quickly looked at Jade to introduce himself. She couldn't press on the fact that something about him carried a difference. Naomi purchased a bag of weed from him. Before he turned to leave, Bags' eyes stole Jade's attention, not his car or what he had. You could tell the life he lived was not the Cosby's, but for some reason, she knew that wouldn't be her last time seeing him. Jade continued working endlessly; however, the hours collected just didn't bring in enough for monthly bills. She didn't like to ask for help from anyone, especially a man, and it had not been her thing to use a person financially.

The struggle felt real though, that one pack of ramen noodles a night, kind of real. She worked for three months, saving only what could, finally able to acquire a privately-owned 2000 four-door sedan. It needed a paint job but the inside looked brand new. The motor must have been no good, because after one month, it blew out, and Jade was over it. Reaching out to her mother, Claudia, she asked if cosigning for another vehicle could be an option, while her father, George, still acted like their child didn't exist. Claudia wanted to try to persuade him before doing so, one last time, as they were paying her car note, adding another bill to the month. Jade never found out what her mother told her father, but shoot her on the right foot, it worked! She enjoyed sitting back in her own driver's seat, rolling the right way, that is with a monthly investment attached, of course. There were no more unreliable cars or hitchhiking for Jade and Naomi, and boy did they roll!

CHAPTER 3

ROUND AND ROUND

They could've rolled until the wheels fell off; however, the more movement or should I say, the wrong movement, brought additional flaws of trouble. Jade was really feeling herself, in other words, doing too much, losing the importance of self-worth and self-respect. A strange number called her phone with a familiar voice on the other end. Jade's ex, Mr. Loverboy T.C., decided to move back in town. She seemed happy and willing to work on whatever the situationship came to be, so Jade located a perfect, cozy one-bedroom apartment for the both of them. The lease was carried in Jade's name alone which allowed T.C. the ability to keep his violent, delinquent life concealed. Being with someone is one thing but living with them can change the whole dynamic. What grew their relationship came from the sex and marijuana that only brought wrongful enhancement. Mornings started off alongside him, eating Jade for breakfast like an All-American platter from Waffle House to where she couldn't help herself withstanding constant arousals.

She loved the feeling of a wet tongue, thrusting in and out, just serving her up and he knew it. Jade's legs would instantly fall, even more to the waist side, as T.C.'s dick rose for the occasion. Grabbing her thighs close in missionary style, pleasing Jade with a stare in the eyes for a strong ten minutes. Only ten minutes. LOL. After sex, they would enjoy a lit blunt most times, which only heightened their toxic patterns of inaccuracy in a relationship. T.C. didn't have employment; that was his good deed for the day, leaving their apartment to run the streets, doing God knows what or who. When she went back home, the duties of cooking, cleaning, paying all the bills, and supplying his needs, were always at the front line. Remembering back during her childhood, things could not be understood about her own parents' marriage; however, we learn these patterns of right and wrong from what is seen, sometimes not intentionally given. Jade never wanted to solely depend on a man financially, but everyone needs help sometimes, and being too independent can also be a flaw when two people are involved. In the evenings, T.C. would return home giving a different mood that changed in an instant, making her feel as if she had to walk on eggshells around him. He became controlling, wanting his decisions of what she should do to become her decisions without question, not concerned with how it appeared—selfish and inconsiderate. Jade realized his actions were only a stepping stool for the physical and mental abuse that, oppressively, would strip her spirit of tranquility.

Alcohol caused a dangerous change in him, and she noticed the need to stop did not come until he ended up, face first, adding his vomit to their toilet after a hangover. Every day their battles of profanity grew louder; the St. Charles Parish Police were getting called out by the neighbors at least once a week. Breakup to makeup was the pull it gave to last that long, and how many of us repetitively do today in our associations. Marijuana only polluted the issues, without depletion. When things were good they were, regrettably, bad times progressed to terrible. Their off-and-on relationship ended again, with T.C. going toward Jade with a closed fist, using height to intimidate her moral confidence. She knew one of them had to go. See Jade also had a temper, and we all know, you can not extinguish the flame of a fire by throwing another fire.

A move seemed imperative so she brought her belongings to a cheap motel on the main road, ultimately, sleeping the entire day away. Jade decided to take a ride for some much-needed time of peace, until she reached the corner store, spotting that same brown Cutlass Supreme she

EEYHNVRTIG : (EVERYTHING)

had seen once before. It was Bags! The eye contact harmonized something serious, it's like their eyes spoke before their mouths could. She liked his demeanor overall; he did not seem too friendly or defensive. Jade had a type and Bags would've, certainly, labeled that. It was easy to accept his advances, being such a hot commodity. It put no restrictions on wanting to be in his presence. Let me explain in detail—he had a caramel complexion with a smile of gold teeth, fine black hair, which matched his chestnut brown eyes, handsome as fuck, and a certain walk that gave pleasing capable. Phone numbers were exchanged this time, and Jade didn't care if he had someone waiting back home for him or not.

They became really cool and were both intrigued by each other. Buying a sack from him made it easy, just to see his face. Jade walked out of Kreams one Friday night and saw Bags standing next to his brown Cutlass. The fitted jean mini skirt she wore gave its own greeting and she knew it, by the consistent stares from men and women. Tempting as she looked to taste, Jade walked toward Bags, who dared to hold a strong will of composure. Such boldness had been automatically seen and felt, with the press of her body up against his, placing a thigh in between both legs. He grabbed her right cheek, gaining the implied consent by a smile from Jade, to fulfill the sexual pleasures of grown adults who, undoubtedly, knew what would begin to occur.

It didn't matter at that point. He wanted to fuck her and she wanted to suck him. They jumped in their vehicles and met at a nearby parking lot, where Bags entered Jade's back seat, pulling her from the front to accompany him in the back. He popped open her blouse, exposing both breasts, but the more of Jade's luscious body he saw, the harder his dick grew in size. She unbuttoned his pants while kissing his neck, before taking it in the mouth for some good ass oral. Slurping and moaning was all Bags heard but he wanted to feel more. As he pulled out a condom, Jade played with her pussy, keeping it nice and moist. Bags threw her head down, ass up to get Jade right where he wanted, teasing her with just the head at first, to completely devour her with himself totally. They had some sweaty, steamy-windowed, car-bouncing kind of sex, that gave him a suited tight vagina and her, the exact motion of a perfect-sized penis. One problem struck the both of them—Bags was not single like Jade, and although that made things difficult, they departed each other knowing that wouldn't be their last sexual encounter.

Whenever an allowed meet-up for him or her paralleled available, what had clearly been understood did not need to be explained. No strings attached! Periods of off-and-on phases would happen as their own lives continued, meeting others, separately. This is when Jade met a new guy named Sean. She paid attention to Sean's funny personality, without really getting to know him or his intentions. Lies were told in ways to get out of anything. After three months, Jade found out he wasn't living with a sister in the projects, instead, Sean lived there with another woman for the entire course of their fling.

In the beginning, he openly told Jade at one point that his participation as a father of five held importance. Round and round, how we keep ourselves stuck in bad situations. Eventually, the news of her being pregnant with his sixth child would produce a change in a different way. It didn't matter what Sean said or claimed to do. Jade's priority stood in the womb of her stomach.

Her First Born

CHAPTER 4

BRANCH BY BRANCH

A tree needs its branches for structural support, like transporting water and nutrients to the leaves. Each serves its own purpose. The family tree is a perfect example of branch by branch. You need one to get to the other, one falls off, another one comes in. In order to continue the circle of life, there MUST be beginnings and endings. Jade knew she would be a single parent. She had to tell her parents and even though old enough as an adult, it still wasn't going to be easy. Claudia showed disappointment while George took things better with time, being her strength of encouragement, to become their family's main support system. Jade worked for a Pepsi facility during her pregnancy, completing factory-type duties and adding countless hours of paid overtime. As long as her movements pertained to the same activities before conceiving, the worry of concern was without need, at least that's what her doctor stated.

One morning, she woke up in a puddle of blood but had no pain. Jade phoned Claudia, needing to go to their local hospital, scared of a physical examination. She decided not to wait for anyone, driving herself to the emergency room, to then see that the bleeding had quickly stopped on its own. Another doctor other than her OBGYN performed a physical exam to make sure the cervix would still be closed, and that she was not experiencing a miscarriage, given the results of a stabilized, five-month term pregnancy. The next few months went by without a problem, until a thirty-eighth-week appointment with her physician for a scheduled routine ultrasound. A report showed an enlargement of the head and medical staff needed to monitor the baby's fetal movements immediately.

Claudia received a call from Jade, informing her of the hospital admittance, which gave a precaution of safety for mother and child to execute an emergency cesarean. Delivered suddenly in the arms of nurses, the infant cried while being taken away to another room. Jade and Mrs. Miller felt something went wrong. With only five minutes to see her baby, Jade was informed of a diagnosis, not familiar, Spina Bifida and Hydrocephalus. The infant had to undergo head and back procedures through transportation with equipment for treatment located at Ochsner's Main Campus in New Orleans. Jade sat in her hospital room, devastated from hearing such traumatic news. Not easily understandable, medical terminology felt like another language. You may be reading this type of information just as Jade did for the first time.

Would inquiring minds like to know?

During the development of the fetus, a spine forms in the first trimester of pregnancy. If this doesn't happen properly, the baby's spinal cord fails to close in the womb, allowing cerebrospinal fluid (CSF) to inflate his/her brain.

There had been no time to think!

First, the back needed medical attention by surgical repair of the protruding lesion, stopping fluid from incorrect transport. After that, in order to drain fluid (CSF) from her baby's head, a ventriculoperitoneal (VP) shunt, had to be inserted on the left side of the brain. This device was able to deposit pressurized fluid through the stomach and into the body system for urinary release.

That is enough learning from Anatomy 202. LOL. Let's proceed.

The separation brought a sense of sadness to Jade. She wanted to be alongside her baby through anything; however, two more days were left of post-op treatment until medical discharge. A few hours later, the doctor notified her with a result of both procedures being successfully performed, gaining admittance into the Neonatal Intensive Care Unit

E E Y H N V R T I G : (EVERYTHING)

(NICU). Parenthood already came with its own set of challenges and daily sacrifices, unexpected medical issues. Now that made things even more complicated for a new mother. Jade finally had a chance to be alone in her hospital room. It all happened so quickly, not knowing where to start but also, too shocked for tears. Videos about the early stages of motherhood were nothing like this. Mentally and emotionally, she wasn't in a good place; the sun was brightly apparent, although, it still seemed dark.

The doctor came in the next morning to check on Jade's physical status. If ready for movement, she would be given her chance to happily walk. All prior conversations from other mothers about how hard walking could be after a c-section did not matter. In order to be discharged, she must walk and that was all they had to tell her. A charge nurse provided assistance by holding both hands, prepared to feel the absence of gravity, she slowly put one leg down ... AND THEN THE OTHER!

At a distance, healing properly through pain and discomfort is how she helped her baby. Jade knew if she could get up once, it would surely be done again with patience. It did not take long for her to step into that mama bear skin and I don't think Jade wanted to jump out of it, nonetheless. On the day of discharge, George drove his daughter home, but once inside for some reason, the depression couldn't be hidden anymore. She cried and cried.

Facing the reality of her first childbirth, she kept blinds to the window, closed to restrict herself from sunlight. Staring at the four walls of her bedroom was much easier than looking at an empty bassinet. While she was under doctor's orders for the next five weeks, the turning point for this somber time started with a refusal for her to face this alone. George began driving Jade to visit her baby. The Millers were greeted and given a brief tour of Ochsner's NICU. Anxious and scared, they knew not what to expect, as wires of technology ran from machines to the inside of incubators.

Each nurse provided nurturing care to another fragile infant, that either cried or looked sedated, in a size tinier than one's hand. In regard to their situation, you know who made things better—the baby, in just its existence alone, the Millers finally saw their bundle of joy and gave much undivided attention. Jade couldn't be more happier to see the one who endured so much in the first week of care. From then on, nothing else was a priority except her baby's recovery. While visiting, she asked questions about things not clearly understood after reading medical documentation and appreciated all moments of progress, however, departure at curfew seemed difficult. Those babies were so sheltered, you needed a code just to begin a conversation with the assigned nurse. Wonderfully established, the NICU's camera system allowed a view of their little one from miles away. The support given by the administrative staff felt unmatched as they gave Jade a gift of medium size, containing books of faith and a beautiful HOPE chain that she easily placed around her neck.

At two weeks with monitoring wires attached, she finally had the chance to cuddle her precious baby while sitting in the hospital's wooden rocking chair. What a beautiful bond! A pediatric doctor moved her baby to the next wing and their situation looked brighter for a soon discharge of release.

THEN GUESS WHAT?!

The infant's back slightly reopened, needing a return for intensive medical treatment. They need to perform back surgery to prevent the risky chance of infection.

George and Claudia patiently waited for both of their arrivals in excitement. Unfortunately, Jade had to break the sudden news, which they were not expecting.

The Millers' wait became longer . . .

Sterile and prepped on the operating table, once more, the surgeon completed another procedure successfully, with the appearance of a corrected skin enclosure. The skin around the site healed exactly how it was proposed in a prognosis, allowing their bundle to be discharged after two weeks of beating all odds. Resilience had a whole new meaning as they acknowledged each hour, starting a new beginning in growth.

WELCOME HOME!

The light of Jade's day and the beauty to all of her nights,

Made perfect to name **her** *STAR**

CHAPTER 5

I AM

Disabilities or special needs can be difficult, there are many spectrums to each condition. Still, you appreciate each given day, with the perception that all children are gifts having a gift. Collaboration takes two parents involved; however, single-parent life is a different type of struggle as Jade had to balance medical appointments for her Star together with job-searching. The Social Security Administration gave her a phone call, bringing beneficial awareness of an accessible income, provided monthly, for any disabled candidate in need of financial support. Jade found a two-bedroom apartment twenty minutes away from her parents and received a permanent job offer shortly after. But like they say, more money has more problems. She purchased a 2006 Chrysler Sebring, welcoming a car note, alongside rent-to-own furniture for her new place, meanwhile, let's not forget the daycare fees that just demolished biweekly paydays.

There would never be enough and Jade did not like asking for help. Payday loans were a scapegoat, so she thought, until filing bankruptcy, that is. Ha ha! Biting off more than one can chew will leave you on a chopping block, if not done correctly. Luckily, she was given a fresh start as her legal issues were cleared. A television broadcast of school enrollment caught her attention between contemplating which bills to pay, possibly being an answer of relief. When Jade spoke to a helpful representative, two programs of education, Medical Assistant and Medical Coding with an Associate's Degree of Science, seemed beneficial in learning more about her daughter's care with a balance of household finances.

Running some errands one day, a man greeted her from behind. It was that reoccurring ex-boyfriend, T.C., AGAIN, who always made you feel sorry for what he had going on. She allowed him back in to visit, occasionally, and of course, Netflix and chill, is what they started to call it these days. In the nail shop, Jade's stomach fluttered enough to recognize the difference from growling. She purchased a pregnancy test which clearly read, POSITIVE! With a fast beating heart, she notified T.C. who wanted her to abort the baby right away in fear of more child support, but that didn't sit right with Jade. After the first scare of an emergency c-section, she worried something might not be detected again. Hoping lightning would not strike twice, Jade made the decision to continue her pregnancy. For better confirmation, she had to be followed by a high-risk specialist and the OBGYN. Although each visit result portrayed a healthy pregnancy, skepticism could not easily stay away.

The second delivery gave a totally different experience, all going just as planned with T.C. in attendance to see the birth of their beautiful boy, Lyon. Jade now had two kids to care for and where there is a will, there's a way—doing it all financially, finishing school to receive a medical office position through externship. In ten years, they were hit with something much harder for them to see. Mr. Miller's health started to decline, causing a weakness in restricted mobility. When the ambulance was called to check his vitals, EMT personnel suggested admittance to the nearest Ochsner Hospital in Kenner, Louisiana.

Due to the results of diagnostic imaging and lack of cognitive brain activity, doctors revealed her father possibly had a few strokes without warning for anyone, including himself. Quickly deciding between occupation or family, Jade stopped working to be available for physician assessments and both parents, in whichever way she could. Household statements were the last thing she wanted to worry about at a time like this. Not sure if unemployment would approve her, as resignation wasn't listed under reason, Jade applied anyway. She didn't have the necessary paperwork, in documentation with detail from a current employer, however, listing the truth about her situation granted an approval. The Miller family arranged hospital visitations every day, meeting providers after daily rounds and participating in treatments for physical, occupational, and speech therapies. As the liver began to notice the absence of alcoholic beverages, his body started going into shock, producing seizures that were only stopped by IV-administered medications. When drinking alcohol routinely for enjoyment, there is a crucial responsibility we must be aware of. Slowly it becomes an unnoticeable craving or addiction that could kill you, without proper treatment, once the body is no longer able to obtain it.

In control of a steady regimen, George made great progress, in a willingness to keep going, and his daughter felt just as proudly motivated beside him. One particular evening after visiting hours, Claudia stayed overnight with her husband to be awakened by him, aspirating on his vomit, causing a restriction of air to the lungs.

Mrs. Miller and the assigned physician called Jade for her return to Ochsner, her father had been moved to the intensive unit, immediately placed onto a ventilator. The accessible machine is a great piece of technology inserted inside the throat's esophagus, however disturbing to see, as that patient is unable to eat, speak, or breathe on their own. During the COVID-19 pandemic, he contracted pneumonia and had to be given antibiotics intravenously for one week, depleting mucus secretions to expand the airway supply of his lung capacity. Jade acted as a pitbull on guard when it came to her father. Through her hardest, the birth of her first child, he was her backbone, and now, she stood firm behind his. While sitting in the hospital room, to keep herself occupied, Jade completed assignments online, helping her gain more medical insight to things she did not understand.

Without warning, she realized that George's bowel movements, becoming very loose and dark, gave a result of vital fluid loss and a need for a prompt blood transfusion. Jade could tell her father felt hopeless as if he wouldn't be getting out of there. Concerned emotionally and mentally, exiting the hallway, she held back no tears. Entering the elevator alone, right before the door closed, an older black minister swiftly came inside, smiling, making a funny remark about walking around such a big hospital. She wasn't big on prayer but gave her name while having a stronger sensation to ask one for her father. He repeated the name and they both exited, going in different directions.

Right before she could reach her vehicle in the parking lot, with tears in both eyes, she heard her name called aloud, viewing the minister so close behind. This startled Jade, as the path he took had a significant distance. By foot, that would have taken him much longer to complete. She walked through Ochsner's main campus, front to back, from many different locations, every day, how could he have gotten back to her so fast?! The kind minister only stated one thing, "Your father will be getting discharged in five days, Blessings to the family," and then he just walked away, silently. Jade said nothing and did not know how to accept his message but it did bring instant relief, lifting her spirits to call her mother before the thirty-minute ride home.

After receiving a blood transfusion, doctors from each medical department approached the family with a treatment plan. If Mr. Miller's vital signs remained stable, he could be released sooner. Since his hospitalization lasted for two months, thus far, Jade and Claudia heard music in their ears and felt no news greater. Results and analysis came back with consistent progression, in which all physicians were pleased to move forward in their decision-making. On the following day, the humble nurse gave Mr. Miller's face a clean shave. Elated, Jade could not stop telling her father about his handsome new look. To her surprise, they were preparing him for discharge. A decision for hospice enrollment had been made in order for George to receive all the appropriate care necessary in a place not only his family preferred, but where he wanted to reside, mattered more.

Terminally ill patients are assisted with medical needs such as daily on-call nurse visitations, prescriptions for comforting induced pain, mindful resources of preparedness, and emotional support for patients and their families. He was home later that evening.

E E Y H N V R T I G : (EVERYTHING)

At this point, George became bedridden and barely able to move, day by day, he started experiencing increased heart rates mixed with fluctuating blood pressure concerns. Symptoms got dramatically worse in the last few weeks of life. It takes a lot to be a loved one's caregiver. Both Jade and Claudia witnessed that. By the start of every morning, Jade arrived for her father's routine care. But on this particular day, February 8, 2021, she stood alongside his bed, unable to get a blood pressure read. As the oxygen machine became louder and three more attempts were made to retrieve her father's pressure, Jade noticed his chest wasn't moving as much.

She called her mother to the room as they

                caught

                        his

                              very

                                    last

                                          breath.

Jade later realized, her father waited to hear her voice one last time **before he seized**.

CHAPTER 6

KNOWLEDGE IS POWER

After Mr. Miller's passing, with extra hours on hand, Jade adamantly decided not to use them for employment at the clinic, instead, she wanted to spend every moment with her mother and children. Leisure for Jade meant ending the day in the comfort of her bedroom, as her children slept peacefully throughout the night. She enjoyed watching Youtube, being able to learn things with just the touch of a button. Strolling through her feed, a lady delivering positive messages while sitting next to a table spread of cards, which she called Tarot, came in between the recommended search. Jade had not seen these types of videos before, nor did they show up. Curiosity struck her to look on when suddenly a card faced the screen as a black and white photo of her late grandmother, Alberta Glossom, appeared. She knew something strange occurred, her twenty-twenty eyesight never left an unquestionable doubt. Speechless without words, her eyes gave some joyful tears.

Startled in her apartment, Jade began to feel chills that made goosebumps arise. She googled the meaning of this since recognizing her ceiling fan spun on its normally, low speed. The advice given online stated, "The divinative presence of outer supernatural activity, trying to spiritually or physically, get your attention." This explanation surprised her to the core, however, she wasn't scared to even know. If that had truly

E E Y H N V R T I G : (EVERYTHING)

been accurate, wondering who it might be, brought sheer excitement. Jade asked, quietly, out loud, **"Is something trying to connect with me?"**

INSTANTLY, a boat behind the levee blew a loud horn giving confirmation. TUHHHH! I mean *instantly*! NO WAY! She stood for a minute, in disbelief, but started to jump up and down in exhilaration. Unable to grasp what she'd just witnessed, the unbelievable, fascinated Jade in her total entirety to know more. Finally, realizing someone was reaching out to her, the next question—Who?

You don't get it. This wasn't some light or strange spaceship in the night sky. That force had to be greatly more powerful to connect in that way with the physical realm. Jade's parents didn't raise her in church, still only one came to mind, GOD.

Feeling overjoyed at just the thought of His presence, she embraced all of the spontaneous activity, barely able to sleep for the night. The next morning, she entered the kitchen and noticed her light began flickering as if to say hello.

Watching as she exited the room, *it had stopped*. When she *re-entered, it happened again!*

Jade's attention, easily given, with a look at the light, to speak in reply. Most people would have been frightened. Not Jade; she truly became intrigued. Wanting knowledge on how to relay a connection, research continued to draw her toward imperative. She began reading about Spirituality, meaning as a whole, we are divine in nature. How awesome is THAT, Jade thought. For some odd reason, the Oneness of our being gave her restriction, for using this, forbade, something not to play with.

Referencing some words not heard of, she recognized the science of energy. In school, we learn it can only be transferred, not created, nor destroyed. Informative literature brought a new thinking of prospection when it came to the energetic force, in the thought of God not being man. Understanding knowledge is power. Jade's spark of interest grew; inquiring a testament about God, the version from the Arabic language, THE QUR'AN, appeared ancient, truthful, and sacred. To solely give all its permitted attention, the decision to wait for purchase came as her online assignments, suppressed an offensive amount of reading. She gained more insight about spiritual practices and wanted to visit a local store in Kenner, Louisiana, named The Witch Depot.

The term Divination had a section by the wall. Jade asked a clerk what it meant, not sure if lack of preparedness stood for an answer. The clerk smiled and directed her to a shelf with boxes, explaining that it is the use of an ability to seek a connection from the unknown, supernaturally. Shocked by the explanation, Jade quickly remembered the lady on YouTube, reading timeless messages from those alluring cards that questionable night. She purchased a beautifully made classic Tarot deck, which included the instructional booklet, for referencing each card and its meanings from directional positions laid upward or reversed. Before placing her energy onto items not known, she went back on YouTube in search of beginner-friendly readings, since looking at the cards meant one thing and using them, spoke another. As she watched on, the storyline of its past events did sound like her own, a feminine made a final decision to end a whirlwind, toxic cycle with a child's father.

Added to the message, is betrayal, linking the ex and family, who were working together to gain a large sum of money by hiring a hitman for a murder plot. A HITMAN! Hearing this information wasn't easy. Jade loved her family. Every day she would watch for entertainment, as the continued invalidness declined false with more truth. After the recent death of a father, property and a hidden family inheritance were supposed to be given to the rightful heir, his daughter, Jade. Furthermore, the reading stated the male had been murdered and a small town community were all in on it. These grew accusations for now. Jade took a mental note while Divination became her endeavor, learning two types, Astrology and Scrying, one at a time. The use of celestial bodies such as The Sun, Moon, planets, and stars is called Astrology.

Scrying, being a term, uses mirrors, water, ink, crystals, and flames, to bring about visions. Born on April 19, she started watching her Sun sign, Aries, to pinpoint certain readings. Jade didn't go by the best background or who had the most likes on YouTube. a Tarot reader named *Goddess*

Energy provided knowledgeable and informative presentations that caught her attention. It would just be her and those cards, sitting in front of a simple dream catcher that hung onto the wall, nothing extra. Her work spoke for itself. Goddess Energy executed a particular reading of a masculine energy marrying an ex, fraudulently, without her knowing, to steal from her deceased father's estate. Every reading Jade watched had many comparisons, in doubt of proof, physically, but mentally, she could not be mistaken about the descriptions of the accurately said messages.

CHAPTER 7

MEANT TO BE

Do you believe in love? Have been in love?

This was Jade's first time hearing about true love in a Divine soul connection. It is when two people are put together by God, who share a soul, destined to serve their mission on Earth. Two people, known as Twin Flames, are the mirror soul of one another separated at birth. Once these souls meet, this sets off a magnetic attraction with intensified feelings from each counterpart. Right away Jade thought, it would be a once-in-a-lifetime fairytale. She had been a no-strings-attached type of gal. Men were only good for one reason—that was sex. When she wanted it, Bags was the PIPE LAYER to handle that service, *easy*. It only took one call, just as simple as that, no questions asked. Throughout the years, they remained fuck buddies trying to keep things on the low.

Bags, being an extrovert, was well-known and lived that street life. While Jade, on the other hand, was a homebody and an introvert. The two were total opposites you wouldn't have guessed it. None of their relationships got in the way; however, she noticed his time became less available. Until they were no longer in contact with one another. One day as Jade was waiting for the kids at school, she sat in her car watching Goddess Energy. The reading abruptly stopped, not allowing her to do anything

EEYHNVRTIG : (EVERYTHING)

to the phone. It's as if God himself were saying, "PAY ATTENTION, MY CHILD." Feeling drawn to look outside, flying in her direction were two beautiful bald eagles one behind the other. Jade was stunned, rarely seeing one, let alone two.

All of a sudden, the two eagles began soaring in a circle above her car! Literally! It was definitely a sign, but what did this mean? After a few minutes, they flew away into the blue sky. Jade couldn't believe her eyes, shocked by this miracle. Equally important, Bags wasn't worried about anything or anyone. He had his own life with a *don't fucking play with me* type of demeanor. Unless about money, he was not answering any of your questions. From childhood, hustling had played a major part in his life; it came easy to him. He traveled to different area codes meeting cartels and drug lords for kilos. Home or away, carrying a Glock at all times was a necessity. If he needed to shoot a few rounds, the task was unloading the chamber on that ass!

When Bags touched back down, Mia would be waiting on him. They had been in a long-term relationship, living on the other side of town together. However, to him, women were all the same and it was second nature for him to drop one and get another. Pussy was pussy! Jade knew of his relationship but was totally taken aback by his actions. Something else had changed and Bags left her puzzled and ghosted. So she did what most do nowadays . . . Facebook. Wanting him to feel a way, she threw subliminals at him regarding his lifestyle. Bags was pissed and threatened her with a sex tape that only he had. To even take it there, Jade became APPALLED! She went back online to throw more dirt on his name. Bags wouldn't tolerate drama, so he cut Jade off completely, BLOCKING HER. Aggravated about the whole situation, she wondered if the readings were more real than the truth could be. Every channel spoke about a feminine energy being ghosted by a masculine energy.

Jade wasn't sure what else was right but had believed she found the hidden link. Another factor in Tarot is Astrology, you would be addressed by sign. The comparisons just kept blowing her away more and more. That's when she first heard of Libra. Jade knew Bags' birthday was September 23, so she looked to see which sign he had. You guessed it—an air sign, Libra. On a conscious level, she felt differently, not understanding why he made such an impact. Jade dismissed the thought as the music started connecting lyrics with life similarities. She needed obtainable information, more in-depth, regarding how a twin flame reflects energy. Jade had knowledge at her fingertips by the touch of a button, Google. The browser stated the reflection of a twin is like looking in a cosmic mirror, searching for your true self.

Since both share a soul, this allows you to target weaknesses and improve strengths that weren't noticed before. In doing so, addressing these underlying issues can provide insight to inner healing and personal growth. Jade further revealed that energies are able to share telepathy, the communication of thoughts or ideas by use of other than the known five senses. Jade just knew an interaction of such magnitude could not have crossed her path. *Or had it?*

A *fascination, full of everlasting love, grew for God.*

CHAPTER 8

SUDDENLY

Change may produce situations that are uncontrollably difficult to handle. Quick to Listen, Slow to Speak, Slow to Anger.

For it takes nothing to put yourself in a strange predicament, be mindful. Jade became preoccupied with the daily topics of Tarot readings, not realizing strength could be tested. Consistent interpretations about an ex knowing of a father's death for money completely triggered her into action. She spotted T.C. at the barber shop, immediately causing a scene with loud outbursts, exceeding profanity. Public attention grew and the authorities were called out to diffuse the altercation. Jade didn't give a DAMN! The Bags situation along with this had all been too much to handle. Police quickly put handcuffs on Jade after hearing details of her crazy accusations. She made one collect call to Bags, notifying him about what had taken place. To her surprise, he accepted while not being persuaded or enthused to help.

Claudia had Lyon and Star as Jade sat in jail for two and a half days before bonding herself out. She began receiving notifications about recent comments on Facebook. It was her so-called friend, Naomi, who had added Jade's mugshot under various older posts insulting her character. THAT BITCH FELT BOLD! Jade wanted nothing to do with her as she had seen Naomi at her worst, remaining a true friend. There was a much bigger threat to humanity in Louisiana than Naomi—that was a hurricane. As Jade began doing online assignments, a breaking news broadcast came upon her TV screen. In the Gulf of Mexico, hitting land in a couple of hours, was a massive life-threatening Category 5 hurricane named Ida.

She anxiously closed her laptop and started to panic. What was she going to do? The meteorologist added that it just so happened to be the 29th of August, the anniversary of Hurricane Katrina. It shook Jade to her core as she googled to verify that date. At the same time, her phone chimed, and without a doubt, a yes confirmation had been given through cellular transmission by God. Jade read writing can be a powerful mechanism for prayer. She leaned on faith, praying for His mercy, to provide storm protection in black and white. The paper was hung on the bedroom wall as she could do nothing but pack suitcases in desperation. On the outside, the wind began to pick up, shutting electricity down for good. Jade's kids became startled as she only had a few tealight candles to place around the apartment.

Cell towers were no longer serviced either, restricting communication to loved ones. She put suitcases on the kitchen table with assumptions of flooding waters as Hurricane Ida made landfall. Soon after, the rain and thunder came pounding the surface while roaring winds caused walls to crack. Jade rushed them all into the bathroom carrying pillows and blankets in hand. The kids were petrified as deafening sounds intertwined with the air-filled snapping of trees, entirely. She heard objects hitting the windows in wait of something coming through the glass. By this time, night fall approached and the pulverizing agitation from God lasted about eight hours in total, then suddenly ceased. It became eerie quiet as the unseen damage wouldn't be discovered until sunrise. Jade and the kids finally came out of the bathroom exhausted and restless for sleep.

The next morning as they opened the door, greenery filled the parking lot as to be a layout of cemented concrete. Downed power lines, uprooted trees, necessity shortages, and waters that flooded homes and vehicles were told in detail. The highway to Claudia's home was submerged, restricting Jade to pass. As she observed the pantry, there had only been enough food

E E Y H N V R T I G : (EVERYTHING)

for two days including one case of water. The summer heat increased during the day and stayed throughout the night. Jade began to worry about the well-being of her kids in such unbearable conditions. A voicemail from her Aunt Francis came, stating the family was welcome to go to Mississippi. Cellular data started to operate, allowing her to check the account balance. Money was there! Star's Social Security had been deposited right in the nick of time. It just so happened that Racetrac, up the street, would be opening early morning and Jade was getting in that line.

After enduring eight hours of sitting, she obtained a full tank, continuously praising God for his favor. This would be the first time traveling without her father to Mississippi by Aunt Francis. Nervous and wanting to beat the sunset, a yellow butterfly flew past her windshield. She didn't think anything of it at first, in her own world, while listening to music. Ten minutes later, in her view, another yellow butterfly had a closeness that caught her attention as it fluttered by.

There was another . . . and another.

The butterflies became noticeably obvious, giving Jade more guidance than the GPS. They weren't on the road alone as it was an incredible nature sign from above through living creatures. Elated in what she had just witnessed, counting each one, provided more assertiveness in the correct direction. Those ravishing yellow butterflies stayed with them the full two-and-a-half-hour excursion. Jade's father, George, frequently made trips to his oldest sister whom he admired most, Francis. Always welcomed with opened arms, her home felt like his favorite. The swift determination of the butterflies brought awareness that someone was with Jade, but WHO?

She had no clue George had been reincarnated by God, directing his family to a known safe haven.

At the exact moment she reached the exit, transformed father flew one last time, across the sign . . . as to say HERE.

The family arrived before sunset and Aunt Francis was waiting for them by the door. With an extra room readily available, Jade and her kids unwinded while Francis prepared a meal. You wouldn't be hungry in her house; it wasn't allowed. The freezer remained plentiful. Jade enjoyed the scenery of a countryside paradise filled with acres of the greenest grass and the tallest trees. She walked along as a field of black and gray feathers stood out in the distance. Spiritually, a meaning once read, they were said to be signs of communication from a guardian angel. Aunt Francis and Jade used the time provided to form a loving bond of togetherness.

Family photos told reminiscing stories that were filled with uncontrollable laughter. During the night, they shared the guilty pleasure of homemade banana splits while watching Hallmark movies followed by interior decorations. It became a much-needed vacation, free of charge! LOL.

Electricity was finally restored one month later back home, though she didn't want to leave. Jade gathered her kids and their belongings, loading the vehicle to full capacity. Hugs and kisses were exchanged as they parted ways, going in two different directions.

Not knowing that would be the last time seeing her face,

                        Aunt Francis *passed away four months later.*

CHAPTER 9

LET THERE BE LIGHT

What if you didn't know you needed to be rescued? Acceptance, we must allow God the closing of some doors in exchange for new doors to be opened by Him. Habits, behaviors, people, including family, and our way of thinking contribute to our day-to-day lifestyle. Reality set in for Jade when she arrived back home. The uncertainties once bothersome before had resurfaced. Truthfulness struck her like a match lighting the way to isolation. There was much progress made in restoration as people returned to the River Parishes community. State agency operations began to resume, including CPS, Child Protective Services. A case worker gave Jade an unexpected visit regarding a report made anonymously. The report stated kids weren't school enrolled and the usage of drugs, marijuana, and Xanax, were occurring in the home.

She did smoke marijuana; however, controlled substances had not been her caliber. Falsification, by fault, was suspected as the case worker contacted school officials to verify placement. With attendance confirmed, the case was closed, sending Jade a determination in letter format. The final outcome is not what the villains craved, placing violated restrictions on her Facebook page gangstalking. A friend request came from a male not known, so she didn't accept, paying it no mind. She began receiving notifications of screenshots from acquaintances showing that the same male had inboxed them. Jade saw the derogatory remarks insinuating craziness and immediately sent a message shaming face.

She was able to tell it had been a woman hiding behind a page; the pettiness was incomparable. The finger bandit insinuated how Jade needed Jesus in her life. It ended with a candle of Jesus from Jade's bedroom, as a responsive, *I Am Here*. They wanted to involve Facebook. Subsequently, she began using the platform as a voice outlet. Defending herself, posts were made about family and frenemies that vigorously plotted agendas. Some feathers had to be ruffled because soon after, calls came in about a fake profile criticizing Jade's picture. Physically, they body-shamed her weight, mocking her facial features of a crooked smile. They targeted another man's wife by uploading their photo to have Jade portray the town homewrecker. While strolling unquestionably, she observed a picture of T.C. and a woman captured "WIFE."

A shock to her, yes, but why hadn't he spoken of this? Jade was beginning to wonder what else he could be hiding. The intentions were not made clear as she made a conscious decision, illuminate Tarot. Whichever YouTube reader appeared, a new line of details sparked interest of an older feminine energy. She poisoned her husband, granting compensation from a life insurance policy while telling the close-minded community that the daughter earned an income from prostitution. Grieving her husband, Claudia grew distant with Jade, not speaking regularly. Jade thought nothing of it at first until she heard the reader deliberate a suspicious CPS case. The altering connection between the spiritual and physical proclaimed a depression too much to bear. Trust represented a losing gamble toward the people she had known since childhood.

In a cold, dark mental state of isolation, all life became insignificant, placing blame atop failure. Jade's internal heartbreak had not been easily seen on her face. Smiling hid the endless nights of tears that interrupted sleep and whelped pillows. The joyous spirit ripped away, making sunlight the burden of proof in the rise of a new day. By nightfall, she would be relieved another day had come to a close, causing the activity of others to lessen. Falling into a deeper hole, mentally, happiness for anyone's accomplishments had been no more. Those four walls became her entrapment, producing thoughts of suicidal escapes from living with fear. A feud began as one side pulled Jade to negativity, not able to withstand the heavenly, sensational Divine support refusing to let her perish.

Supernatural experiences weren't accepted when voiced. She couldn't speak to anyone about the forbidden combat, except HE. One sad morning, the outburst of a loud cry mixed with an unconsolable flow of tears had filled the room. As she sat alone at a breakdown moment, God chimed the phone, and she felt an embrace hug being given. Jade realized there was a reason to live on Earth and this would not be the defeat if God hadn't come for her soul.

In the same way as a product is set with an expiration date when made, He has put forth a provision for ALL. As people we must take part in the choice, of life or death, by not giving up, nor should the decision be made to forfeit our destiny.

> The Most High has given mankind of the living, **Free Will**— the ability to do something at one's own deciding discretion.

CHAPTER 10

THE BATTLE

What we do in this physical realm matters. Mankind and the universe are connected as a whole to solidify a justifiable balance. Constitutional Laws are legalities, Universal Laws are principles based on rights, ethics, and morals of the human being nature. Energy is converted into your Karma, good or bad, depending on which side you prefer. Have you ever had a time when something felt boomeranged back? I'll wait . . . There is no such thing as coincidence! Everything happens for a reason. Just because you don't know it, doesn't mean there isn't one.

In a relationship, people don't see what conspires behind closed doors; however, it is seen and all darkness comes out, eventually. Mia, Bags' fiance, would constantly look at his phone. In doing so, she found out about Jade through text. She was not intimidated by anyone Bags slept with but his actions brought worry unspoken for. When asked about Jade, he went from being quiet to bashing her during pillow talk to convince Mia otherwise. Bags had been mistaken. Mia's suspicion increased as she took a deeper look inside of Jade's life. Mia kept things hidden about herself. She was into the Practices of Evil by drawing upon Dark Arts. To find out needed information, they would secretly use Tarot as a Divination tool for inspection. Mia grabbed a personal deck asking questions about Jade— THE LOVERS card immediately landed on the table. This infuriated Mia, slamming a glass against the wall. She didn't like being notified that Jade was Bags' counterpart Twin Flame. Refusing to let this happen, she devised a disturbance plan. Clouding Bags' judgment would be first.

Mia begins to tell Bags that Jade uses Black Magic to refrain him from her. During the next Full Moon, she performs a confusion spell, loudly chanted, to cloak the energy. When energetically something is made completely invisible to the naked eye, this is called cloaking. A confusion spell would keep Bags under an illusion about Jade while preventing her own deviant character from emerging in the physical. Mia needed someone who knew Jade; someone close enough to get her out of the picture, totally. She went online viewing T.C. on her fake page and desperately wanted to speak with him about a financial murder proposition. After receiving the inboxed message, T.C. realized Mia and Claudia had much more in common, a systemic hatred for Jade.

She expressed this to T.C. a month ago before George unexpectedly passed away. Both women spoke briefly, arranging a meeting with T.C. later that night. In the local cemetery, all three produced a coven, pledging secrecy for the devil's contract of Spellcasting and a hunger for murder. Claudia had the money to pay a hitman, T.C. knew of some funny moving people, and Mia's crooked family worked in the legal judicial system.

Tired and ready to go inside, Bags pulls home to find Mia sitting at the kitchen table with glee. She tells Bags that there is a hit on Jade's head for 20,000 and he must be the hitman. In this line of work, Bags had no problem accepting a job but Jade . . . he couldn't. To add more fuel to the fire, Mia wanted him to prove his love by killing Jade himself. Not trying to answer, Bags changed the subject to who wanted Jade dead in the first place and how she knew.

With a sinister smile, she told him the word around town was someone named Claudia needed this done. He walks away quietly. Unexplainable feelings made him ghost Jade; now, he HAD to stay away for her safety. Mia did not like his response as she threatened to kill Jade if he goes anywhere near her. Claudia was perpetually good about keeping this sadistic side of her cloaked by only speaking to Voodoo priests overseas, not in the

THE BATTLE

states. Now that she had the house to herself, every night the attic would be the place for her nightly rituals of witchcraft. Dark curtains were draped around the windows as tables were filled with collectible jars of chicken feet, animal blood, potions, and skull-lit candles. Claudia read a death spell, in tongue, off of the altar while burning each picture of Jade and her kids, one by one.

After Jade and T.C. broke up, he and Claudia remained in touch despite Jade's knowing. She was able to tell that T.C. had been an energy vampire, able to deplete joy from another human being. In previous years, he sold his soul to the devil, participating in a blood sacrificial murder, to become a warlock. He felt comfortable enough to disclose this to Claudia but what a careless mistake that will be. This became an advantage, adding him to her twisted plot of obtaining generational currency. Empowerment framed Claudia's face by the definition as a scheduled unorthodox meeting back at the graveyard was set for 3:00 a.m. They passed the gate entrance, marching in black-hooded robes, wearing upside-down crosses around their neck. Claudia retrieved virtuous information from the priest combining Necromancy, an act of communicating with the dead, with Black Magic for a heightened accrue.

T.C. and Mia held hands in a circle hissing around the mound. Claudia tasted the worm-filtered soil before placing enormous amounts into a locked wooden box. Ignited to please The Angel of Wickedness, she tilted her head back laughing as the ignoble would. The conjuring enactment began to corrupt Jade's dream state—a shaded-black demonic spirit approached her. In that instance, God awakened Jade. Not understanding what had happened, she denied sleep to go on Goddess Energy Tarot on YouTube for an explanation. She delivered a message of concern to a Divine Feminine regarding Black Magic coming from a Karmic Feminine. Jade learned these titles recently online, as they didn't label her prior to, but it did explain the nightmare-ish attack. Who could want to attack her, spiritually, she thought, and why?

The Tarot reader continued, the Karmic Feminine wanted the Divine Masculine to herself while getting rid of the Divine Feminine in any way

EEYHNVRTIG : (EVERYTHING)

possible. Jade sat on that knowledge and the next day, she kept seeing Raden's name everywhere she looked, on TV shows and movies. Raden was Bags' real name. Jade hadn't been able to make the strange connection. A dream sent by God hit her like a lightning bolt that showed images of Jade and Raden with romance. Dreams were not seldomly coming to her before, so there had to be meaning with purpose. Elated with the thought of Bags, did Jade just get guidance from God of who the Divine Masculine is? That's a strong YES!

The dream had also triggered her. Bags' silence left her furious and in doubt if he was involved. All Jade could remember was him threatening to do something with her sex tape, not putting anything else past him. Facebook started to be her new avenue for giving unknown enemies a piece of her mind. She opens up, spilling the tea about Black Magic being done, and purchases a copy of THE BOOK OF SHADOWS. Jade knew nothing of magic, but posted the book along with his home to show it as a weapon of protection against whomever had been linked to Bags. Mia decides to use this as her opportunity, pointing the finger of craziness toward Jade while saving herself. Disgusted with Jade's entire soul, having outed her truths, she began twisting their destiny for success. Mia became her doppelganger, the copycat, by starting a YouTube channel with Tarot to seem innocent of cause. The exclusive channel would allow her face to remain secretive, restricting any leads of worriment.

In figuring Bags saw things her way, he no longer viewed Jade the same, any communication was unwanted. Evil felt in control of the physical and increased daily Spellwork to consistently harm in their benefit. Digestible foods, including liquids, are practiced by sorcerers to hex individuals, stopping any goodness in vitality. Mia begins submitting menstrual blood as an ingredient to red spaghetti for the curse of Bags' misconception.

CHAPTER 11

GOOD VIBES ONLY

The foundational core of your happiness can not depend on others. The Self, contains the rising internal endurance to heal transmutable negatives into positivity.

Self-love became a premonition for Jade when she started to look toward The Almighty and not man. A ray of burnished Sun had shined on her as she drove to an urban shoe store, The Source. Jade walked in and was greeted by the captivating sound of a masculine's voice in a symphonic, melodious language with passionate fervor. She glanced up at the television and saw an opened book with obsolete colored pages of a script different from the one she had seen. The YouTube icon was visible but Jade wanted to know what it was and the meaning behind it. An employee by the name of Hum De, retorted with a forthcoming gratitude of praise in record of this book, called THE EASY QUR'AN by Imtiaz Ahmad. He had a strong Arabic accent and was readily honorable of his Muslim religion, to imply.

As Jade noticed his eyes fill with water, a beautiful explanation began, describing his faith in Allah and moreover, how He sent this Book from the Heavens for mankind and jinn. He encourages her to read this Book daily, if only, the smallest portion of a verse or page at a time. She hadn't been guided to read a biblical testament before but with the message so clear again, instantaneously, the purchase was made on Amazon, viewed as the first option. Jade didn't want to read another book alongside this one. Attention fully given in a quiet space, having no distractions, and a Jesus candle lit, the process had begun.

The meanings were a necessity. She wanted to understand what Allah and his Prophets iterated by comprehending subtitles to chapters known as Surahs. Just because you are one nationality or religion does not mean inspiration of another is unacceptable; skepticism of truth for Jade failed to appear. The guidance stuck out like a sore thumb, as to be the manual of life given to mankind. Allah became the importance on all levels of commitment, learning how to feed the soul by fasting and starting a journey of celibacy. She walked away from everyone for the cleansing of her own energy and enjoyed peaceful moments in nature, watching signs of His presence.

The struggles of life had not ended, and money was insufficient as Jade defended the motherly role, prioritizing financial sacrifices. One unsettling factor hurt—the agonizing realization of her needing to pawn items out of the apartment to purchase diapers for her son, Lyon. She pawned a Samsung Galaxy tablet reaching just enough cash to split between two ways, diapers and fuel. Jade's relief lasted for a minute, certainly missing the test of what transpired. Allah provided the two obligatory needs manageable for the next few days. The chore of washing clothes needed to be done, so she walked to the laundry room of the complex with a basket in hand. When Jade moved the mountain, high clothes from in front of her face, a filled table with stacked diapers all Lyon's size, had sat there in wait. She grabbed them quickly, bringing all the packages inside but did not recognize God's graceful compensation.

God moves in ways we are unable to understand. His continuous action is not halted by sight, but that speaks of the characteristic trait of sovereignty based on Him, not ours. One way in which you can't refuse is that *Right In Time* moment when there can be **no** such dispute of His name, said repeatedly then. Jade had always felt in control of things with independence; however, by going through this trial, she learned that there are some you can't control, but Let Go and Let God. Peace and a relationship with The Creator became a practice of the consistently needed acknowledgment in her life. There had to be a choice in change made within, the gain of patience and self-love. When a person decides to work on the internal issues that are based on past experiences or childhood, this can promote healing and relay care of endearment.

The healing process is difficult, but just like a wound has this encounter, so does a person, in order to improve. Jade was more concerned about herself eternally, not just physically. The full transformation enabled the aspect of being grounded. Mentally speaking, grounded happens to be the ability to stay calm about who you are in those times of uncertainty.

In those times, your energetic vibration can ascend, go higher, or descend, go lower, bringing you to a new level of classification in the aurific field. Jade started to understand how accurate energy had always been after the combat of depression that could no longer keep a stature of low vibrational energy around her. By inspiring her own improvement, God aided in locating the origin of authenticity.

She presented better decision-making with the use of discernment, to judge things in perceivable measures clearly including intuition, for those not obvious. This meant the openmindedness of understanding as focus on retaliation prohibited the necessary offerings toward forgiveness. When you're in that egotistical mindset of wanting others to suffer, there is always going to be defeat aimed at one's own peaceful consciousness. Allowing this wall to combust enables your sanity of the present and releases any past resentments from people or places keeping you in a tedious requisite. Instead of pointing the finger, recognizing your own faults may take time, but once seen the criterion, back-up-of-failure, becomes an interruption.

Jade apologized to God first and foremost, then to herself, further stretching to others with heartfelt words of emotional compassion. After that, there was no turning back. She had finally become her second fan as the known fact of the first lie with God. Not in a sign-your-autograph type of way, but in the STRONGEST magnitude of motivational support to never give up and keep going.

The truth remains and it will evermore stand until the test of time,

                                        God Loves All Of His Children.

CHAPTER 12

ONE SMALL MUSTARD SEED

Jade heard of the word Faith, but had not fully understood the preeminent meaning or the total involvement of resilience it took to keep it. She did notice it was like an activation of belief in God and his majestic omnipotent powers, during all times good or bad, sustained in the smallest size. God is always near, never far, and the service to him began in the comfort of her own home. There had been no distance between them. The praised acknowledgment could be seen or heard wherever, not only in the Home of the Gospel. She went without a selection of church or religion, remaining true to Him with integrity, as the different religiosities gained respect by contribution. In looking for a sermon to view one Sunday morning, The Duplantis Ministry aired on local WGNO, invoking a glorified message.

It became the joyous, informative way to retrieve God's words as immaculate grace, humor, and truth had been given in constant stride. Jade repeated daily obedience advancing inspiration to more, watching prophetic movies with fellowship, and praying enchanted scriptures. This does not stop the enemy from manipulating you back to old patterns by infusing toxicity into your path, causing destructive embarkments.

T.C. and his wife, Pamela, devised building a future with arrogance and pride as false pretenses were aimed at Jade for fun. They didn't mind starting inappropriate conversations about her. In fact, it made their day to know others were entertaining gossip, whether true or not. The community looked at Jade differently and T.C. knew people would not care where or how she went, out of sight better for them.

One thing about him, nothing had been safe. He couldn't hold water even if it inhabited his last ounce of survival. Wanting the fame of a rap career badly, T.C. felt the ultimate way there would come from, boasting in secret about diligent organized crimes. He created a mixtape in the studio about two plots intended for Jade, as Pam smiled with the encouragement of a new radio hit. The ranted killing of his two-timing baby mother being shot by a paid hitman and the forged identity for substantial life insurance claims. Pamela heard T.C. making a call to someone named Mia stating what perfect time it would be to let them get acquainted. Through comparison of interest, another hateful spirit is added to the bunch, all willing and ready to see Jade unalive. T.C. made Pam aware of a planned courtroom injustice, that he and Claudia had underhandedly needed her vindictive participation in being Jade's doppelganger.

She couldn't get prepared fast enough, sliding on a black wig as to practice for a full screen, Fine Arts Broadway. They went to the Justice of The Peace to forge official marriage documents, by using Jade's stolen identity. Once the murder of Jade and her children was successful, T.C. and Pamela would legally be able to collect subsidies from life insurance. What Jade didn't know was that T.C. had gone into her purse, stealing older cards of her personal identification. He wanted money but ever since word got back to him about Bags and Jade's affair, an ending for her was the only alternative. Claudia stood to meet Pam in full satisfaction of her partake in completing the alleged scheme. She called Mia and Pamela over for some tea, to give yet another bargain with criminal mischief spread widely across the table.

Legna Mortgage allowed Claudia only 40 percent of the property estate owned by George, so she made a check to Jade as if to receive anything, not bringing suspicion. Mia practiced signing Jade's signature and put on a similar disguise of her appearance. Claudia instructed Pamela to attend, giving both the check, in an urgency to cash at a particular bank,

StockFarm. With an innocent smile grazed across her face, Mia walked to the next available bank teller named, Scott, pulling out the financial check and Jade's driver's license. The male teller declined the transaction as he looked at the expiration date, punching a hole for future indication that it was not to be used. She grabbed the card, in a joking manner, stating her current license was in the vehicle. Out the door, Mia went but never returned.

Scott had been confused by such odd behavior, although, deciding to make a mental note of the incident, he continued assisting the next customer. Mia and Pam were embarrassed to inform Claudia that the card was now made useless, and the mission would not be completed for anyone's safety. Claudia scolded the both of them, yelling words with profanity as she requested Pamela and Mia to leave. This wasn't the news she expected and hearing Jade's name pissed Claudia off to a maximum boiling point, where phone calls were started to ruin her daughter's reputation. She made a heated call to T.C. about Jade being a terrible mother, having an STD from her prostitution lifestyle and spread the word. T.C. went to anybody who had listening ears. If they couldn't, he typed it for them in text messages and online platforms.

The rumors multiplied quickly; everyone was talking, plus Naomi wanted to get in where she fit in, so she called Bags merrily, confirming Jade worked the streets. Bags acted like this had been no bother or shock as he played his part becoming an open enemy to Jade. All the slander made it easier to label her being a downgraded, psychotic bitch that needed to be locked away in a mental institution. Homeboys and family members told him to stay away from her because Jade wasn't to be trusted, wanting only his money, practiced Voodoo, and carried diseases. Apart from his stretched bloodline community ran many relatives. This remained not known to Jade but T.C. and Bags were fourth cousins.

She would deal with both periodically when desired. Bags knew about T.C. keeping it secretive; however, T.C. later found out through gossip. Consequently, T.C.'s skin-deep envy for Jade's cheating amplified the betrayal yet he never said anything of this knowledge. He rather

E E Y H N V R T I G : (EVERYTHING)

covertly planned in the background against her, by arranging ingenious counterplots with Mia, Pamela, and ringleader, Claudia. There was another undisclosed fact that people hadn't been aware of—Jade's biological mother died during childbirth, forcing Claudia's stubbornness to jealousy as the Evil Stepmother. At a problematic time in their marriage, George cheated with an ex-lover, Serenity Harris, born to the higher bracket family of society, and conceived her first child.

She moved from Louisiana to New York only coming to visit for work purposes, but ran into George along the way, rekindling a long, returned spark.

After the death of Serenity, an inheritance was given to him for their daughter, Jade. He placed this information in the will that Claudia forbiddenly changed. Preparing herself for wealth, she acted as the loyal wife, remaining close to murder George and Jade, while taking full ownership of the entire estate. Jade began focusing on herself but continued having vivid dreams, not able to interpret what revelation had been shown to her or God's necessary meaning behind them. The dream revealed Jade's father suited in a dark-colored military uniform, signing documents in an office, sitting with joy and nobility.

Enamored by the connection of detail, she intermittently felt an extreme importance in following <u>all</u> of The Creator's indispensable counsel of guided perception. Jade put both, the visualistic images from Him and Tarot together. Some may question this forsaken aspect as being partitioned with the Evil attributes of Satan; however, she thought, well if this were true, couldn't the Light side's illuminate powers invade darkness, deserving supernaturally given worthiness? Isn't there right and wrong, that can be done using almost everything in the world? What you do with the admission of it is the cautionable problem and God is the omnipresent one to fear. It became Jade's outline to combine her subconscious and physical realities. She prayed for enlightenment, asking angelic forces to send protection before each Tarot reading.

Three cards that quickly landed on the table were *Death, Ace of Cups, and The Emperor.*

CHAPTER 13

10 X FOLD

Divine's pressurized time was torturous, as Mia disregarded not hearing a final job of murder, stopping Jade's life. She goes through the lengths of Tarot to discern if Bags plans to kill her, or any feelings he may possess related to such nonsense. A question given aloud caused the swinging out of The Empress card and the Ace of Cups, firmly. Mia couldn't desist the fumes of melted clothes onto her burnt flesh from heated rage, in relation to Bags' audacity. When The Empress falls out, it speaks of a feminine energy inheriting strong, nurturing maternal skills influenced by romance, business, and intellect. The Ace of Cups is withdrawn as a great omen for such new beginnings in love, deeper relationships, intimacy, and compassion than ever before.

This extracted answer made very clear proof to Mia that Bags would never kill Jade, so she now wanted bad blood from both of them. Bags was bombarded by Mia questioning the type of day he had, though her interest caught him by surprise, he didn't make any assumptions about the strange behavior. She decided to take a different approach stating, "The fly on the wall has a better chance of surviving than Jade, anytime your own mother wants you dead."

Bags asked doubtfully if the lady named Claudia was Jade's mother and why did Mia second-handedly leave that crucial part out, as her mystery transcript. There could be no answer from her, just the shrug of shoulders added with an extra threat of telling Jade everything he had done. Even as Bags thought walking away showed less care, Mia knew the undying truth of his heart, and she began to plan death over life.

She calls a cousin in the police force to get personal contact information for a previous supplier, long rap sheet Lucifer, the city's biggest Kingpin. He didn't talk much on the phone but Lucifer wanted to see her in person, so they met at Lakeside Mall. Mia tells him about cashing $15,000 to help set up a robbery on Bags and whatever else they see to take is theirs. The two have made history off of successful revenue from drug trafficking back in the day. Lucifer wasn't going to turn money down for an easy job and he didn't like Bags running shit in that part of town, getting respect no way. Writing their address with feelings absent, she desperately included the different times of Bags' arrival, throwing in which neighbors to be aware of. On the scheduled day, Mia slipped two Valiums in her man's glass of Crown Royal and Coke in the refrigerator, as it patiently waited for his indulgement.

Sexual relations were easier locks to get Bags prepared, as she did the same to arouse him, wearing lingerie in their bedroom. Mia spoke to him, not verbally, but the opening of her thighs insisted his firm dick of erotic pleasure, causing Bags to sleep without worry. Slowly the gang of Lucifer crept to the back door, which Mia eagerly left unlocked, giving access for their unexpected entrance. Dressed in all black and wearing white masks, they quickly ran into the bedroom, two holding AK-47s, and the third covered Bags' head with a pillow, pistol-whipping him profusely. The gang demanded all of his money, beating him unconscious, randomly, knocking items to the bloody floor. Mia screamed, playing a cry for help, only to signal the consented slap bruised across the higher right portion of her face.

With crocodile tears, she smiled in excited delight as they took off running through the back door, then bailing in unmarked cars down the winding street. In this life, police were never called. You handled it your way—your terms, no questions asked. Bags did not suspect Mia, but when no one else was home, he placed two hidden cameras in the living room and kitchen for his own security. The information regarding who participated in this home invasion would come around eventually, when Bags least expected it.

Pamela and T.C. were busy trying to keep their marriage intact. Money became a lesser option due to Claudia's financial downward slope of currency. An eviction notice was taped across their door for other tenants to see and the decision to move had come right behind it. The apartment smelled terrible with brown packed boxes, cockroaches that were alive or dead for months, and nothing to eat but expired cereal on top of the refrigerator. Pam decided to take a nap as her hand grazed across two phones for T.C., stuffed in the living room sofa. Breaking his code to the suspicious one, she goes through text messages to find Na-HOE-Mi and T.C. were meeting up often, having sex. Pamela should've been focused on her own relationship instead of jumping on a three-wheeled bandwagon for Jade, recognized by the scratching of her irritated pussy.

An appointment was set for a routine gynecologist, where positive blood results of contracting HIV were given to Pam, who then screams horrifically. Naomi had many encounters without protection. T.C. wasn't the only one. He also didn't mind letting condoms gather dust in the back of a wallet.

As tears pounded down Pamela's face, she loaded some of her boxes into the vehicle, leaving abruptly in a combative mood. When T.C. finally gets home, he notices the emptiness and a handwritten note is left for him, enclosed three last letters from Pam, - - - - - - - - H I V.

Shocked and worried at the same time, T.C. gives Claudia a phone call notifying her of the crooked fork that's been thrown in their path. They weren't sure what heartbroken Pamela had up her sleeve. The involvement of Claudia's desperate scheme pertained to all of them. Locating Pam's whereabouts was of more concern. She reached out to Mia to give word in case Pamela contacted her for anything. Beginning to quiver from a bad feeling of reversed Karma, she runs to the attic on bended knee, pulling clumps of hair from the head.

E E Y H N V R T I G : (EVERYTHING)

    Energy has to be balanced, spiritually and physically, and actions will remain justified as God has placed unbreakable humane laws for the entire universe. In unimaginable comebacks to defeat the wrongdoing, His universe retracts energy back TEN times stronger, annihilating deception in the physicality of mankind.

    This is the meaning of tenfold: Be careful what you manifest for another. What goes up must always come down.

As Above So Below

CHAPTER 14

LOOSE STRINGS

- The tightest group can become unthreaded, even when you think success is accomplished with 'the more the merrier.' Throughout my years, I have heard someone is always watching. That continuous message didn't include who, however, His silence is no longer mistaken and please know ALL will fail, indefinitely. -

Mia couldn't believe how well Bags maturely accepted the robbery but satisfaction for her would be controlling the sequence of events until the end. After searching online, she purchases a tracking device to place under the back tire flap of Bags' car to know his location every time. While he took a shower in their bathroom, Mia ran outside, glancing around for a second, to then connect her new profound entertainment. One night, Bags decides to take a curious ride before going home, innocently, passing through Jade's neck of town. Alerted as a new destination, Mia receives this on her phone and calmly begins to drink, while thinking a setup with heroin would strip Bags of freedom.

He pulls up in the driveway being greeted by Mia, as music blared, grabbing his gun to exit the brown Cutlass. She isn't hesitant to seem erratic at this second because the need to get in that car, secretly, is the ultimate goal. Hugging him, they walk inside one after another. Bags goes into the living room to roll a blunt, while Mia felt the timing called perfect for her malicious gratitude of, "I got you now." Placing heroin in the appropriate compartment of his car, she walks back inside ready to release tension, saved from that apparent joy ride.

Mia's demeanor changes instantly as the door slams with her return. Plunging to their sofa, she hits Bags to start a violent altercation. He pushes her off of him, smashing the room table and causing cuts to Mia's left arm from the broken glass. Running to get a bat out of the closet, she swings directly at Bags, striking a hole in their busted wall. He realizes that sheetrock was almost his head; he then grabs Mia, choking her by the neck, raising both feet off of the floor. Kicking the stomach of Bags with strong blows to get loose, she spits in his face to show full-on disrespect. Red fury in the eyes, he gives Mia a well-fortified, backhanded slap to the mouth, causing blood to leak from two sites now. She runs to the kitchen, as it all worked out her way, to call 911 in tears, crying for help from the domestic violence of an abusive lover.

The police get there in no time and the role Mia plays is close to winning a Grammy award, screaming PLEASE from the inside for them to move faster. Bags wasn't too concerned since he hadn't started anything, but his claim of self-defense did not match the wreckage scene. In handcuffs he went, as the smell of marijuana floated in the air, to Mia adding his placement of stashed heroin in the locked middle console. It didn't matter what Bags said to the cops. They were done and all he saw was them taking a small sealed package out of his car. The question of pressing charges is asked, with an officer's writing of a documented police report, as Bags is driven away straight to jail. Mia walked inside the damaged living room, lighting that same blunt, smiling, not worried about how much time he could possibly get for this backstabbing plan.

Bags is booked in the McKinley Correctional Center for heroin drug paraphernalia and a domestic violence charge with an appointed court date to stand trial. As there was nothing to do but sit in a cell, aggravated, the iron-framed door opened, letting a familiar Rex inside. Bags grew up with

Nick Turner, better known as Rex, back home in their small town and he knew all the street gossip, real or fake. Rex told him the streets are talking, saying Mia set that robbery up with Lucifer's gang last week to demolish his credibility. Facts were facts to Bags and this wasn't one to him. He chuckled, as the thought of Mia's unloyal con had been dismissed, running in and out of his head. It was normal for them to fight from time to time but taking it that far could mean she set no boundaries when it came to messing over him.

Mia had everything to herself, running things at home, driving Bags' car with male passengers, supplying drugs, and smoking up all his weed. There was something else she became fond of doing—credit card scams, using another's personal identification, to accumulate their consistent flow of cash. Mia communicated daily with a hacker named Tek-e, who would give a database containing Social Security numbers of deceased holders, remaining untraceable.

One day, she uses the identity of a well-known politician from another state to apply for a credit card application online. This flags an awareness alert to the US Department of Homeland Security which opens up a fraudulent investigation, contacting local authorities about an IP address listed under Mia Collins.

Detective Theodore Hoffman was assigned the case, retrieving anything linked to Miss Collins, starting with bank accounts and widestream devices from her location. Hoffman notices text message communication in the current feed, with a Claudia, discussing if the visit to StockFarm had been finalized. He calls the bank to obtain a history of her transactions, to find out she has none, and some questioning in person was shortly decided vital. Arriving at StockFarm, the detective is greeted by compliant Scott, who is the first person he informs of the open investigation regarding the activity of a suspicious female identity fraud. Scott easily remembered that mental note of a woman trying to use an expired driver's license in hopes of cashing a check, as he directed Mr. Hoffman to their side office. With permission given from his supervisor, Scott locates the entries input that day, along with the security cameras' video footage.

Detective Theodore has a picture attached to her folder, as the video shows the appearance of a different woman, clearly wearing a short black wig. Further investigating the details and time of visit, they were able to see the check was from Legna Mortgage, made to Jade Miller. The detective takes this information to report criminal perpetration to other bureaus for their tedious documentation.

Rearranging her bathroom at home, Jade was surprised by a visitor knocking on the door, Detective Hoffman, with a badge in hand. He begins to ask if she has issues with the use of her driver's license, and provides a warning for the attempted identity fraud pertaining to Legna Mortgage.

Detective Theodore wasn't sure of Jade's position in the alleged scheme, not wanting to speak about the credit card investigation until seen necessary. She knew nothing of the company but wrote down the name, thanking his service. With a business card quickly given, he said he would be staying in touch.

The Great Almighty dismantles most thought of plans in His time, by releasing various **loose strings** to appear suddenly, an unmatched Supreme like no other, with masterful powers of vengeful delight.

It didn't take long for Jade to prepare them all for bed that night, as a dream came to her, showing Bags with an injury to the right hand, wrapped in white bandages. She woke up confused by what this meant because they no longer spoke by contact. Looking like the untrustworthy one to Bags, Jade kept this to herself. Seeing his face while sleeping and not being able to touch him triggered her. She downloads an app called Text Now and begins sending obscene messages to get Bags' attention, in the worst way. The messages didn't get to him until he received credit for time served equivalent to three months. He was released from McKinley on a six-month parole probation. Bags' release from jail was a big shock to everyone including Mia. She had the weirdest smile on her face when keys slid through their front door, showing his unanticipated return.

Mia greets him with no empathy but decides to say something related to the way Bags miraculously came home too damn fast. He goes to their bedroom, checking his phone before a shower. Unfortunately, he locates the disturbing messages sent to him by unknown numbers from Jade.

Declining to reply to say a word, he blocks all of the numbers instead, not able to get over the hurt-filled betrayal with words continuously. Mia had to run out for some quick errands. In a hurry, she left inboxed emails logged into her open laptop for Bags to see one odd subject. He wanted to see what "The Composure" was about and found it to be a group message sent from Claudia Miller with two added recipients, T.C. and Pamela Cox. As he knew Claudia for being Jade's mother, Bags couldn't believe the murder hit on her life had been placed right in his eyesight, through email. It showed the others were involved more than he thought. Bags held onto this information and started keeping a close eye on Mia, as sexual activity became less. Realizing her gestures of fulfillment have completely stopped with him, increasingly mad from rejection, Mia plots a killing not escapable.

She calls T.C., telling him Bags is reacting differently and that they have to get him out of the way, sooner than later. Mia allows T.C. to hide in the room across from their kitchen, wearing brass knuckles and a sharp butcher knife in hand, ready for the surprise elimination of death. Tracing Bags' route on her hidden device, they knew his exact time of entry would be in their favor, if done correctly. The security camera was not set with a chime for notification in secrecy, it only showed when Bags went into the software. When she sees his car pull up, Mia grabs a meat cleaver to put downward in the back of her stonewashed, blue jeans. Nothing is said as he walks in this time. Going toward their hallway, Bags is struck in the back of the head with brass knuckles by his jealous cousin, T.C.

With her knife raised in the air, Mia leaps from the kitchen, stabbing Bags in the right hand using all her strength to inflict pain. T.C. tries to zip-tie his hands but the left-handed jabs aimed by Bags make it complicated for them to control the irrepressible situation. Refusing to exit without a fight, he uses his knees to roll from under both Mia and T.C., making a speedy run through the blood-given path to his Cutlass. Bags throws his ride into gear, looking at the steel gun on his passenger seat as the smell of burning rubber followed him down the street.

He leaves town ghosting everything, as it was no longer safe for Bags to trust anyone, anymore.

Mia cannot believe they have let Bags get away. Losing her mind, she desperately watches Jade's Facebook profile to see if the two, are speaking... again.

CHAPTER 15

THE REUNION

The successful assassination had gone terribly wrong. T.C. wanted his face to be the last thing Bags could distinguish but now getting to Jade, certainly, was the new threshold. Taking the loss out on her, he purchases a gun from his homeboy, Cap, and decides to plan a gang rape, damaging Jade before a close-pointed shot. Cap didn't know her but he knew people, so for $5,000, she wasn't going to be classified as a problem in his existence. T.C. doesn't have the money. Deciding Claudia would be honored to pay, he calls her with the detailed plot and the missing whereabouts of Bags.

Claudia wasn't impressed with the hitman being a previous lover to Jade but hearing about the rape gave some new hope for her final resting place. She gives T.C. five thousand, as time was beginning to be pressed, telling him to come back only on the account of speaking news that he has promised. The call is made to meet at Kreams. Cap and T.C. talk for a moment ending the conversation with the pass of money by handshake. An untrue person doesn't realize the astounding fact, that they are dealing with people just like them, deceitful.

T.C. was not seeing movement in the plot of Jade, but those three letters left by Pam were haunting him every night through nightmares, subconsciously. It's a dangerous game of carelessness out here. HIV is easily passed from carrier to carrier. He wanted to know but refused any medical treatment, hoping no news is good news.

Bags travels to the northern part of Louisiana, paying only cash for motels, remaining under the radar so no one would find him. He even left his cartel supplier without telling him a word. That was breaking street code to Lucifer. This had to be the reason to kill now.

Deciding not to check into a hospital, Bags wraps his right hand in white bandages and begins to monitor the hidden cameras at their home. He notices Naomi, T.C., and Mia talking in the living room about arson, planning to set the house ablaze for insurance money. Bags wanted retaliation on all three, so he followed his intuition, saving all recorded video footage that may be needed at a later time.

The universe continues its reign of Bad Karma, strategizing with energy while they plotted. Naomi had not been told that SHE was becoming the talk of the town. Everyone that Naomi gave to was feeling symptoms of fatigue, infected blisters, and burning sensations with their sexual organs. T.C. wasn't having these problems but that was a part of his given dose—the notion of not knowing, that he too, contracted the Human Immunodeficiency Virus.

Meanwhile, Cap decided to make some money at their local Walmart, when he gets busted with his third strike, selling two ounces of marijuana to a customer outside. He was going to be facing three years in jail unless he made a drastic move, and tell them something they would want to know. As they look at him with a tap of the finger waiting, the sudden words about a five-thousand-dollar payment for a gang rape slowly came from his mouth. Detective Hoffman wanted more information regarding who their target was, the responsible parties, and if he still had the money in his possession.

An answer was given with a bending of Cap's back to reach for knotted cash out of the left shoe, to then slam it on a table, saying the name, Tylor Cox.

Leaning in the chair he said, the person T.C. requested this for was Jade Miller, one of his baby mothers, whom he grew to hate. Hoffman needs to complete a statement. Pressing the recorder, Cap gives his full name,

Aaron Jacobs, repeating truthful details once more of a heartless crime. The detective doesn't see a terrible background, but Tylor didn't have a permanent location and he wouldn't be easy for them to find. However, the female's name rang a bell—Mr. Hoffman had just met her one week ago; first, the suspicious activity at StockFarm, and now this excruciating circumstance.

Jade was too busy following the guidance given to her by God. She cared about His views or what He could be telling her with stern importance. In using Tarot, a new term, Karmic Masculine, continued diligently working with a Karmic girlfriend of The Emperor, planning to kill him by unexpected stabbing to his death. Even though Jade wasn't able to talk with Bags, there had been an overwhelming concern about his safety that restricted her from letting it go. She tried to warn him, repetitively, not worried about how it looked to anyone else. Jade wanted Bags to know the danger around and it did not matter who could've been a villain.

Monitoring the latent security cameras became a part of his daily routine, watching day and night as notifications of detected motion were being captured. He sees Mia in the kitchen removing a bloody tampon to allow the digestion of a clot by tongue, then she smears it over her face and Bags' picture, chanting sinister words of Evil torture.

The relationship had already ended with his ghosting when they tried to kill him, but all of the blindness turned into concrete evidence that was only contained by him. He felt sick to the stomach, imagining what else could've been true about Mia or what else he had completely wrong regarding his views on Jade's spirituality. Bags also didn't feel any remorse for his cousin, T.C., as he joined their tasteless revenge to receive the ultimate punishment of underhandedness.

Detective Hoffman began investigating Tylor Cox by locating a phone registry from AT&T, contacting the department to maintain an incoming and outgoing communication log. A number listed with Mrs. Claudia was seen invariably too many times, where it grew questionable suspicion, further noticing the duration of each call. Searching for more of her information, the detective wanted to utilize a permanent address with ownership to Claudia Miller, which made an eyebrow raise, giving familiarity.

As she slowly went along the path from her mailbox, an unmarked white vehicle pulled into the driveway, asking to speak for a minute with the information about someone potentially dangerous. Claudia's oppressant home had not looked or smelled inviting; however, that wasn't worse than the eerie-insensitive feeling Detective Hoffman identified. The information, briefly stated, was someone by the name of Tylor Cox, may be charged for an indecent crime, and they needed to find his location. He politely introduces a question about their relationship and the length of time they have known each other.

She gives the biggest grin while stating he is the father of her grandson who stays in touch and is always welcome to call after parting ways with her daughter, Jade Miller. Detective Hoffman paused his writing, since the name was heard before, then continued, "Would you or Jade know where Mr. Cox would be found?" Claudia tells him she has no current address and Jade has chosen a type of lifestyle she doesn't agree with, so they don't speak often. He thanks Mrs. Miller for the patient details given, adding, hopefully Jade's lifestyle isn't illegal or he could be looking for her next. She watches him leave, then slams the door, beginning to panic, regarding just how much the detective really knows that he may be withholding.

Later that night, Jade gets a banging knock on the apartment door, and in nothing flat of a second, jumps to look through the peephole, seeing no one is there. It wasn't easy for her to shut her eyes after that mysterious visitor, but she eventually managed to fall asleep. With errands to run the next day, Jade walked to her car when the greeting of a man startled her from behind. He had on a dark baseball cap, wearing shorts, and a white tee, constantly peeping to see if someone followed him. Jade noticed the man was carrying a gift bag in his right hand that resembled the same wrap of white bandages she curiously saw in a dream. As his hat tilted to the side, Jade stood totally shocked at a bearded face, staring into hers, with the point of a finger signaling an inside entrance. Jade went to unlock the door, when instead, he stopped her from opening the door, using no key at all. She didn't even know how to perceive that; it veritably showed his type of life in a bombshell, but what Bags had to say *would be unforgettable*.

Before Jade could say anything, his pupils flooded with water, putting the hand up to start first, finally ready to get something off of his chest. Bags began saying how sorry he was and things had not been easily seen, adding that she wouldn't believe they wanted to kill her for $20,000. He heard about the hit from ex-girlfriend, Mia, who said, in the beginning, a woman wanted this done for no particular reason. When she realized he wasn't going to do it, Mia threatened him by saying she would if he didn't stay away from Jade, so he did. Next, Bags told her that Naomi called with a rumor of Jade prostituting herself and that pissed him off while being disgusted, nonetheless. This was the reason why he didn't care about the vengeful act of exploiting her body, with the masturbating sex tape.

Not knowing what to say, Jade blamelessly sat as a tear began to roll against her left cheek. Bags puts his head down, giving awareness to the hurt he caused her, but there was more that had to be told. The visit could not last long, however stating Mia and T.C., tried to kill him in their home by showing his right-handed injury. They jumped him from the back as he walked through the hallway. T.C. hit him with brass knuckles while she continued stabbing him repeatedly. Bags tells her there is something he must do but support from Jade is needed to give him overall confidence in achieving it.

She promises all that, thanking Bags for his truth and appreciating every word spoken. Bags ends the conversation by saying that they are to be in no contact for everyone's safety and not to tell anyone anything about their meeting.

He decides to make the biggest move by informing The Federal Bureau of Investigation, not his local police about both death plots.

Number 15 was the intended chapter for events about to happen.
In Numerology, number 1, defines fresh starts with new beginnings,
and number 5, stands for universal transformation of change.

CHAPTER 16

TRUTH BE TOLD

The temperature in Lucifer's blood kept rising; the tension angry enough at Bags to kill, with the one in mind he could easily find, Jade. He was going to lure Bags out of the shadows, indisputably, bringing a guilt of despair along for the danger in her life. A ring of Mia's cell phone causes Bags to view his camera. He hears Lucifer's voice on speaker, mentioning Jade's name. Bags had not gone against him and didn't plan to, but messing with her put a dead ass target on the Kingpin's back that would end his whole pharmaceutical street game. Making his final decision, he receives a returned call from an FBI agent, wanting to speak personally and directly. He drove cautiously to the station, meeting Agent Max Frost at his office, given details by witness account. Agent Frost is speechless that Bags knows all of this essential info including his, without unreasonable doubt, evidence in emails and video recordings.

They shook hands, with Bags sliding his real name, Raden Smith, confirming the work of an informant as the envelope was stamped, CASE. The local police department is prepared to accompany the FBI on one of the hugest cases in Louisiana by opening a full investigation. Without revealing this case to the public or Jade, they began to monitor her movements and others, putting spy devices in unknown places for her safety. After seeing "The Composure" email, first, Agent Frost goes for the weakest link of their group, Pamela Cox. It wasn't hard to track her down, viewing Pam's cell tower, a location pinged at the Red Ruby Gentlemen's Club. In casual clothes with a badge in hand, Frost stops Pam before entering her car, asking if she could meet him the following day.

When Tylor Cox is mentioned, Pamela's eyes turn red with envy, giving her account of being his victim of HIV. She pulls something black out of her purse, the second phone not known missing by T.C., gladly able to provide Frost with more evidence. Pamela just tells enough to save herself, illegal stories of crimes once told to her, even the mixtape, were coming out. What had been offsetting to Agent Max about this phone was the language T.C. used in the text messages. They were showing the actions of a murderer. He also found communication in the calendar regarding the business of making and selling counterfeit one-hundred-dollar bills to someone named Naomi. Without telling Pamela what he knows, Agent Frost inquires about Claudia, described as a kind older woman who recently lost her husband. The interrogation is over as he closes his manila folder and walks Pam to the door until further assistance may be needed.

All of this hidden background work about Jade, in the physical, didn't amount to the beautiful futuristic revelations sent by God in her dreams, keeping consistent awareness of His power. She was greeted by a black male who walked with her through a well-lit home, being acknowledged as many people of color in all black, had smiles adding the word, congratulations! When they entered a bedroom, there was the naked body of T.C., lying on his stomach in bed, having a strong decomposing odor, and showing only the waist down. The male told her that an investigator who was making rounds was going to the homes of others, but would be coming to Jade's door very soon. She woke up having so many feelings of amazement, wondering if those supportive people were, ancestors, who knew her by glimpse of sight.

As the song "Groove With You" by The Isley Brothers played, a four-door white Crown Victorian with dark tint pulled into her apartment section. To her surprise, it was Bags, coming to tell her about some undercover work he would be doing for a friend. Bags gave a smile and openly stated that when he was done, he would be back but the time wasn't known. Remaining preoccupied with cleaning out her purse, Jade saw that white piece of paper appear which she wrote Legna on, fall to the floor. She decides to call Legna Mortgage to ask if anything had been written in her name that she should know about. A phone representative politely assists Jade with her account, informing her of the check for $2,000 placed in Claudia Miller's hand one month ago.

Instead of mentioning an issue to the company, she calls Detective Theodore Hoffman to ask how she could go about pressing charges. Detective Hoffman steers her away from the thought of pressing charges just yet, as the FBI already made local authorities aware of fraudulent activities. Hoffman contacts Agent Max Frost to join in agreement with partnering up for the investigation, both giving their part in evidence.

The officials began comparing their evidence linked to the crimes of one person, Tylor Cox, and going through Facebook was the task for them, hoping to find his location. An active green light showed recent online activity, so they searched his identifiable data to locate the IP address being used. Walking out of a pawn shop, T.C. is greeted by three officials wearing guns and badges, firmly telling him they needed his answers to their questions.

T.C. was left seated in a mirrored room while they gathered files and evidence to authenticate the investigation.

Beginning with the press of record:

Detective Hoffman: What is the relationship between you and Jade Miller?

T.C.: What do you mean? There is none. We just take care of our son, that is all.

Detective Hoffman: Would you happen to know of Jade being put in any danger?

T.C.: Nope. (*He shakes his head.*)

Detective Hoffman: The witness account from Mr. Aaron Jacobs, may say otherwise. Does 5,000 sound familiar?

T.C.: Am I arrested? *(arrogantly speaking)*

Detective Hoffman: Maybe, we have found a lot of interesting factors to your way of living, Mr. Cox.

T.C.: I don't know what you're talking about.

Agent Frost: Well, let's talk about something you do know. *(placing the phone on their table)*

Detective Hoffman: Still quiet, I see. You're a different person when you are making music as you have much to say, then.

T.C.: How did you get my phone, man?

Agent Frost: We're asking the questions here! Do you want to tell us about "The Composure" email from Claudia Miller?

Detective Hoffman: Or should we ask your wife, Pamela Cox? Who isn't too fond of you right now, anyway.

T.C.: *(starts to sweat from hearing their evidence)* It wasn't my idea or money! Claudia wanted Jade dead. She hated her and that bitch deserved it in my eyes.

Agent Frost: Mr. Cox, it isn't like you haven't killed before or have tried to recently. Does Raden Smith ring a bell?

T.C.: Yeah, that's my cousin, but he was fucking my son's mother! Maybe you should ask him about her.

Agent Frost: We needed your statement on Claudia, but there is an excessive amount of charges that you too may be facing.

Detective Hoffman: So start from the top. We don't have the time to sit and look in **YOUR** face all day.

T.C. felt pressure escalating upon him, telling them everything he knew was the only alternative. The officials finally received details regarding their elaborate mission, but they wanted the true motive behind the envy of Mrs. Miller, the killer. Going toward her with a different approach, taking Agent Frost along this time, they relay her identity has been stolen by perpetrators, and they need a given statement at the station. Claudia politely gets in their car, clueless, stating how much she appreciated the work they were both doing, addressed as, God is good.

By record of her voice, the two men sat, separated, from Mrs. Miller.

Detective Hoffman: Is there anything you would like to say before we get started?

Mrs. Miller: No, sir, please proceed.

Detective Hoffman: We have recently been told that your hatred for Jade Miller can not be wavered, at the least. Why is that?

Mrs. Miller: I can't believe you could suggest such nonsense. My daughter is all I have after my husband's last breath.

Agent Frost: Oh, it's nothing like that Mrs. Miller, please keep your composure, or do you just prefer the word usage for one's email subject?

Mrs. Miller: (gives blank stare) I'm unaware of what you are implying. I usually don't communicate through email, but someone else could have?

Agent Frost: (snaps his finger) Almost had it. Too bad for you, the email was sent to three other recipients, two, we have already spoken with. Let's cut out the Mrs. Elizabeth act from Young and The Restless!

Detective Hoffman: We also have the $5,000 you paid for the alleged gang rape on that one person left, who you dearly love so much. *(shows small size using finger and thumb)*

Mrs. Miller: Yes, I loaned T.C. the money but he told me it would be for his new apartment, needed after the separation of their marriage.

Detective Hoffman: You seem to be real friendly with money, how nice! Have you assisted Jade and her kids financially? Or is that where your going to say $20,000 **HIT** six months ago?

Mrs. Miller: (eyebrows turn downward) I think I'm done answering your ridiculous, choice of questions, and there is nothing left to say.

Agent Frost: (bangs the table with both fists) That is probably the best thing you could've said this whole damn time. We have what we need for now, but don't worry, I will personally be looking into your ass. You better pray I don't find anything else.

(Both officials get up to leave and a name is yelled across the room.)

Mrs. Miller: Mia Collins! She was the one who wanted my child dead, all because of some man named Bags. You two should arrest her while I call my lawyer for this lawsuit. *(said with attitude and the fold of her arms)*

    Claudia didn't care about anything but herself. Even her employed staff of criminals would not know, they were going down, alone. Instead of calling her lawyer, she informs Mia as if to give a warning for unwanted guests.
    The recorded call was heard by the wiretap placed on Miss Collin's phone after Raden's judicious confession to FBI Agent Frost. Mia hangs up the phone in a panic and begins to pack her bags for the great escape, not wanting to get entangled in their spiderweb. She heads to a gas station

E E Y H N V R T I G : (EVERYTHING)

for fuel without noticing the vehicle that trailed behind her. Finishing the transaction of cash inside, Mia walked toward the door to see her car missing, no longer at its gas pump. When they see her screaming, the disguised vehicle pulls up with two police officers who handcuff Mia, bringing their assailant downtown. She had not sat still like the others, so they let her feet rest in steel chains under a wooden chair to prevent movement.

Agent Frost and Detective Hoffman enter for the interrogation.

Mia: Where's my *fucking* car?! I haven't done anything!

Detective Hoffman: You're being recorded, so we suggest you calm down. The owner of the vehicle, Mr. Smith, has it in his possession now.

Agent Frost: He is a living miracle after the two of you, one being his cousin and the other an ex, tried to stab him to death.

Mia: *(leaning forward)* I wasn't about to keep letting him beat my ass and it isn't my fault. He gained another enemy by sleeping with the bitch, Jade!

Agent Frost: Jade Miller seems to be the common denominator of everyone's problems, but all the evidence points to you! Mrs. Claudia Miller has given us supporting details about your part in planning these apparent murders. *(using them against each other)*

Mia: *(not able to show anything but anger)* What! She's lying! That backstabbing cunt was the one who came with emails and a pissy check for us to cash at StockFarm.

Detective Hoffman: Who is us? You were the only one seen on camera footage in the bank. What could you add in that we may not know?

TRUTH BE TOLD

Looking at your credit card applications, we might be calling you the wrong name. *(said jokingly)*

Mia: Pamela Cox was with me when Claudia gave me the check to cash. She waited in the car outside! I guess the camera didn't pick that up. *(rolling her eyes)* Well, since all my shit is out. What about the false marriage T.C. and his pretty wife put Jade into for a life insurance profit?

Agent Frost: We spoke to the recipients of that "Composure" email but we need proof of what you're telling us! Trust and loyalty aren't something either of you have in your vocabulary.

Detective Hoffman: Where is this documentation? Why did they want Jade married if she isn't? There has to be a better motive behind this than what you're stating, and we're getting tired of everyone's hamster wheel races.

Mia: Claudia has it somewhere in that dusty ass house, stuck in the attic, where she practices Evil spells of Black Magic.

Detective Hoffman: (opening his laptop to play her famous kitchen video) Is playing with your menstrual blood while screaming a chant not considered the same?

Mia: (becomes unhinged, spitting and kicking her legs, only to move nowhere)

I'M NOT GOING DOWN FOR ALL THIS BULLSHIT!

Agent Frost: You got that part right, not going down, **you're already there**, get ready *buttercup! (as both men leave suddenly)*

A search warrant is arranged to get into the home of Claudia Miller, but first, they decide on using their governed resources for a detrimental ordinance.

CHAPTER 17

LIBRA SCALES

Physically we may or may not see the penalties or punishment of one's crimes, however, the true representation of Justice can only be given by Our Judge, God. Enabled belief in him provides a swiftness toward faith, when you're made aware of his omnipresent domination by immediate command Here and The Hereafter, nothing is *forgotten*. Agent Frost openly discussed his need to contact The Department of Treasury with Detective Hoffman for an original will of George Miller that may be on file. They were able to locate Mr. Miller's will and told Agent Max an envelope attached with the name Serenity Harris would be mailed to him overnight. Frost had not recognized the name but wanted to know her connection in this as he patiently awaited their mail on the following business day. When the file is retrieved, he remained sitting, shocked to witness an account for Jade Miller's biological mother, Serenity Harris, was incorporated in the father's original will, without Mrs. Claudia Miller anywhere.

Does Jade even know that Claudia is her stepmother?

Agent Frost was not comfortable telling Jade until he could give her documented answers obtaining the truth, but rather impelled to inform Detective Theodore of their next move.

While in police custody, Mrs. Miller knew the two officials were going to be using a search warrant to raid her home. As Detective Hoffman passed through the garage, he noticed an attic door, still, slightly propped open, expanding his curiosity. Claudia's attic looked like a dark dungeon from Hell, with altars draped in skulls and mason jars of labeled Spellcasting ingredients.

On the side of Jade's family picture lies a book of contact information for overseas Voodoo priests listed next to the word, Hex. Detective Hoffman almost busted his face from sliding down the frail attic stairs to show and tell Agent Max what he had frighteningly seen. At the time of intercession, Frost located a folder in the computer desk of Mrs. Miller's living room, covering that Legna check and George Miller's supposed will. They head back to their precinct, reviewing the case, with Pamela being next to capture for withholding information and the falsified marriage of Jade. In order to hoax Pam into coming, Detective Hoffman tells her of a reward she is to pick up for the arrest of Mr. Tylor Cox.

Greeted with a smile given by the officials and pointed to their interrogation room, Pamela rises up for the entrance of Frost as he places her in handcuffs, without hesitation. Over an airway transmitter, an arrest is made of a female, Naomi Jenkins, who tried to use a counterfeit one-hundred-dollar bill at the Foot Locker in Lakeside Mall. Agent Frost recalls a conversation through text messaging in T.C.'s illegal activity phone and wanted to speak with her at sudden arrival. Naomi watched the clock for thirty minutes until Frost and Hoffman questioned her about which associations she may have links to that could run new leads. Threatened by her background plus their faces, she throws in street gossip confirming the robbery set up for Bags by Mia and her drug lord, Lucifer. She also tells them that Lucifer started using the abandoned warehouse on Main Street for drug trafficking and due to Bags' silence, he planned to kill Jade, too.

Hoffman decided to look into Lucifer's background and his last release date. Strange coincidence, the judge that set him free was Mia's uncle, Benjamin Collins. Frost schedules twenty-four-hour surveillance at Main's warehouse, hoping to arrest Lucifer and keeping him off of the streets for good. When two vehicles enter the garage for a long period of time, S.W.A.T. and The Drug Enforcement Administration raid in, collecting ten kilos of cocaine wrapped inside five rusty, oxidized cylinders. Dangerous Lucifer is escorted to the office of Detective Hoffman and assures all details of Mia paying him to rob Raden Smith. They wanted to know more of her associations, so Frost made a call to Verizon for a copy of Mia Collins' phone communication log.

One number particularly stood out because it began with an area code from the western part of the United States, ending with one-minute calls every Thursday and Friday. Frost didn't need anymore to know if they were being investigated, so he gave Mia her phone to answer the suspicious ring. The one-minute call is completed and an email from Nova Co. subjected, new fashions, came in with a list of the ten deceased to be used for credit schemes. Hoffman was able to track down their designated IP address, while Frost recognized the location as being a hotspot from a previous bureau case. Watching this person's online trail of illegal activities, they find out his name is Wei Sung, criminally known as Tek-e. FBI and local police suited with guns surround the residence before sunrise, busting door frames to locate the crafty hacker enclosed inside a room wall.

Back to their collected evidence, Frost dials a number of an overseas Voodoo Spiritualist in that book out of the attic, asking about Mrs. Miller's desires in service. Erosive Madam had not gotten paid; however, when the call was answered, she paid Claudia back by telling Frost the truth about poisoning her husband for money. Frost recorded their call and began inquiring about her performed task of service, spiritually, which she wouldn't be comfortable exposing to an authority figure. Madame added one more grave detail—Claudia's wishes of death and hatred for her stepdaughter, Jade, were given as consistent reminders every phone call. All of the information lined with Mrs. Miller's deception, so Frost compared both will documents, noticing the differences completed by her falsification. Hoffman and Frost went over their case one last time, deciding they finally had enough answers to let Jade know everything, without question.

Two men dressed in black business suits were motioned on camera walking toward Jade's door as she quickly rose to answer them, remembering her dream of an expected FBI investigator. They introduce themselves, firmly stating that Jade needed to come with them right away to their headquarters regarding her and the kids' safety. Luckily, she was home alone because the kids were at school, so it seemed perfect to leave, not knowing what they could be telling her. When they arrive, Jade is seated on the opposite side of Agent Frost and Detective Hoffman in a small room having a one-door window. Frost pulled out his manila folder with their evidence, telling her about the fraudulent crimes of stolen identity theft and their attempted murder for hire.

Hoffman grabs another folder showing a list of perpetrators, the pursuit of gang rape violence against Jade, including knowledge of a reliable witness that became an informant. Documentation of their hospital visit, proof of her biological maternal parent, Serenity Harris, and George Miller's original will were also given to the victim. She could not fathom how these things were happening without her discernment, but there was an immediate gratitude for the willing participant, who risked their own life to save hers. As Jade opened the room door, viewing the hallway lobby, she spotted Raden smiling, reaching an upright position wearing a nice black and gray tailored suit.

A smile from Jade is returned before she takes off running to leap in his arms, thrilled to see him after six months but happier by the moment of truth.

They walk to an isolated corner with tears in Jade's eyes. Raden informs her of the coming trial that they BOTH will have to **testify** for.

CHAPTER 18

NOW YOU SEE ME, NOW YOU DON'T

Due to the severity of the case, Jade is told by Agent Frost that she is to have no communication with Raden Smith for their own security during trial. A wallet carrying a different identity is shown as an acknowledgment of the words, "Witness Protection Program." Detective Hoffman states that day would be both hers and Raden's opening start. One police officer gathered some belongings to reach an isolated location with Raden. Another official brought Jade to her designated address for twenty-four-hour security of government protection. The trial is starting in one week. Both plaintiffs have set appointments to meet their lawyer, Mabel Stone, to go over their evidence and court proceedings. Mrs. Stone has made a career prosecuting defendants, in federal and state, for fifteen years, deserving a reputation for Victorian success in five of the worst criminal cases served in Louisiana.

Providing their funding for basic needs, US Marshalls would also have to escort both plaintiffs to their destinations until the trial completion. A trial by jury is appointed to Judge William Patterson, a war veteran deserving an honorable record for integrity, courage, and his patriotic service, in the representation of our country for twenty-five years. Detective

Hoffman and Agent Frost speak with Mrs. Stone to verify that Plaintiff Raden Smith will be the first witness to testify against Mia Collins. As Judge William Patterson swears in, anxiety for the case set into motion for everyone's entirety. Nothing but whispers could be heard throughout courtroom walls.

Mrs. Stone, the prosecutor, cross-examined her client, Mr. Smith, stating, "Weren't he asked to murder a lover, Jade Miller, for money and did Miss Collins threaten to complete this herself?"

Mr. Smith replied, "Yes, Mia Collins, told me a woman named Claudia would pay $20,000 for a shot to the head and if I continued seeing Jade, she wasn't scared to have blood on her hands instead."

Mrs. Smith paused for a second, "So when you decided not to fulfill this, is this when Miss Collins, tried to stab you to death inside the home with your own blood relative?"

Mia stands up in court to shout, "He is lying!" (*while giving Raden a look of demise, but is interrupted by the judge to have a seat*)

A smile came across Mrs. Stone as she stated, "Please relax, Miss Collins," then began to present her crucial evidence, playing video footage with audio of Mia running from the kitchen swinging a meat cleaver in the air.

The jury gasped in surprise for Mrs. Stone to add, "How great technology can be when it is used properly, and if Mr. Smith added cameras before or after the alleged robbery?"

He replied, "After, but initially, it was for home protection, I didn't know just how valuable they would become in my fight for life."

"So you weren't made aware of this setup being staged by Miss Collins and her dear friend?" *asked Mrs. Stone.*

"Excuse me, I should've known because someone did mention it, through the grapevine, but I quickly dismissed it even being true at all," *Raden stated as he gave a look down.*

EEYHNVRTIG : (EVERYTHING)

(The courtroom door opened, with one bailiff escorting Chester Martinez, better known as Lucifer, to a seat wearing orange clothing and handcuffs on his back.)

Mrs. Stone began cross-examining the defendant, "Welcome, Mr. Martinez, let's make this short, shall we? Did you participate in the robbery toward Mr. Smith and were there any other extracurricular activities against anyone else?"

"Yeah, I did it, but the crazy part is, I got paid to do it when I would've done the job for free." *Martinez smiled in his generosity.*

A recorder is pressed by Mrs. Stone with two people, Mia Collins and Chester Martinez, having a conversation about killing Jade due to Raden's irresponsible disappearance.

Agent Frost soon walked in before their second victim, Jade Miller, as she was guided to a seat next to the plaintiff's podium, across from the witness stand.

"Miss Collins, why is it you deny knowing our female, but clearly pretended to be her at StockFarm, wearing a black wig?" *stated Mrs. Stone.* "Please tell the court your full intention, maybe I'm missing something."

(There is nothing but silence given from Defendant Collins.)

Mrs. Stone adds, "Since you refuse to say it, I don't mind assisting, your strength to do these things may only show up behind the walls of a business or inside the home, right?"

The jury is presented with a two-part video revealing a crime committed by Mia attempting to cash a check under Jade's name in full disguise. Evidence on the footage, secondly, showed the defendant in her kitchen doing Black Magic, smearing menstrual blood on pictures of Jade and Raden.

"HOW DARE YOU!" *Miss Collins scolded.* "Your days are numbered!"

Judge William Patterson hits the gavel for an order in the court, regarding her immediate threat and sign of disrespect. "If that is done again, Miss Collins, there will be a new charge added to your list of indecencies. This is my courtroom!"

"Thank you, your honor," *said Mrs. Stone.* "I would like to examine two individuals that would, unfortunately, have to be seen at different correctional centers, digitally."

"Hello, Mr. Tylor Cox, please grace the court with your presence. I would like to ask some questions pertaining to the case," *Mrs. Stone stated.*

(The unshaved face of Mr. Cox was then uploaded on the oversized computer screen for all to see.)

"Is it true, you plotted along another defendant, trying to kill Mr. Smith in his own home, hitting him using brass knuckles, while he got stabbed continuously?" *asked Mrs. Stone.*

Embarrassed as he looked to be seen in the faces of Jade and Raden, his given answer of disgust, "Yes, but he is still here, ain't he?"

As Mrs. Stone smiled at Raden on the witness stand, "Yes, we must thank God for that!" "However, Mr. Smith never expected his blood cousin would've ever been a willing participant in releasing him from life."

This did not feel like music to Jade's ears. She just heard the father of her son, Lyon, and the one she truly loved were related, but no one said a thing.

"Please tell the jury, why you were so adamant to complete such a heinous crime, Mr. Cox? If there is a reason to give at all!" *said Mrs. Stone.*

"He betrayed me by sleeping with my son's mother, and thought the streets wouldn't speak of something, he could not," *answered in a deeper tone by Mr. Cox.*

Inquiring quickly, Mrs. Stone asked, "So, is that why your hatred for Jade Miller grew to the point of paying someone $5,000 to commit a gang rape violence against her, before ending her, too?"

Tylor said, "Yes!" *firmly while the audience replied,* "Wow!"

(At this point, Chester Martinez is escorted out of the courtroom and Pamela Cox is zoomed in for Mrs. Stone's litigation.)

Defense attorneys had no choice but to sit and witness all the tangible evidence given in court by the plaintiff's legal team.

"Good morning, Mrs. Cox. Let me know if you are not able to hear me?" *greeted Mrs.*

E E Y H N V R T I G : (EVERYTHING)

Stone, as Pamela shook her head for affirmation.

"Have you been married, once or twice, Mrs. Cox?" *petitioned Mrs. Stone.* "You do know one marriage is allowed at a time in the United States, yes?"

Mrs. Stone gave Judge William Patterson two marriage certificates with distinctive, handwriting similarities.

An answer of "Once" *is heard from Pamela Cox, as the lawyer advised Mr. Smith to switch seats with Jade Miller, putting her on the witness stand.*

"Hi, Miss Jade Miller, it's been a long time coming," *giggled Mrs. Stone.* "Would you please take a look at the certificate on the right and inform everyone here today, if that is indeed your signature?"

Looking at the computer screen and her attorney, Jade answers, "No."

"I rest my case, your honor, there are no further questions regarding that matter; however, I do have one last defendant to introduce to the court," *Mrs. Stone said.*

(An older black woman with bulging dark eyes and short gray hair is presented to the court.)

"Mrs. Claudia Miller, so nice of you to join us. I'm sure the anticipation was **killing** you, but perhaps not, seeing only YOUR corrupted endeavors pertained the word," *Mrs. Stone added.*

"I do not recall what you are speaking of," *stated Claudia.* "I would never hurt anyone!"

"No, Mrs. Miller, most mothers do not, instead we are a part of the strongest protectors in our society, but you're ... different," *the legal adviser declared.*

"The interrogation was interesting, but not truthful. Mrs. Miller, you stated the $5,000 you gave Mr. Cox had been for a new apartment, correct?" *implied Mrs. Stone as she questioned.* "Mr. Tylor Cox, were you moving anytime soon, or did you tell Mrs. Claudia what the money had been for?"

T.C. felt the heat coming off of Claudia through the screen but gave an honest reply, "Yes, I told her exactly what I needed it for."

(At the witness stand, Jade drops a tear of expression from listening to all the truth about everyone's individual role.)

Mrs. Stone became concerned for her client asking, "Is it okay for me to continue?" *(Jade shakes her head.)*

"Judge Patterson and the jury, I have uploaded an email on the screen, 'The Composure,'" *pointed out by the prosecutor.* "Please, take your time in reading this while it is explained."

(Claudia begins to tap her left foot.)

"This email was from the IP address of Mrs. Claudia Miller and sent to the other three defendants you see here before us," *added Mrs. Stone* "They were going to murder the plaintiff and her children, collecting from life insurance policies."

"It is not against the law to get policies on your family. That email has been tampered with, Judge!" *yelled Claudia Miller.*

"Silence!" *Judge Patterson demanded as the gavel came down.* "Proceed, Mrs. Stone."

"Yes, your honor. Mrs. Miller pardon me, but you are not in authority to speak of what the law is," *claimed Lawyer Stone.*

Agent Max Frost provides a manila folder to their case partner.

"Was the law in your hands, Mrs. Miller, when you fraudulently falsified a documented will signed by Jade's father, George Miller, and Jade's biological mother, Serenity Harris?" *frustratedly implied Mrs. Stone.* "Why haven't you told her you were the stepmother, all of this time, or has your true motive, just been revealed?"

"I . . . " *stated Mrs. Claudia Miller.*

"You what!" *stopped by the plaintiff's attorney.* "I'm sure the court and myself are completely done with your lies of deception, but since your will to continue has not seized, let's . . . "

Mrs. Stone turns to Mia Collins, "Did or did not, Mrs. Miller ask you if there had been someone that would kill her dear daughter Jade for $20,000?"

"Yes, we ALL wanted her dead!" *said Mia as she leaned in closer.* "Claudia hated the ground she walked on but tried to say it was me, alone."

"You weak BITCH!" *blurted out the ringleader defendant.*

Judge William Patterson sat red in the face, "One more disrespectful outburst like that and I will have you removed out of my room for Contempt of Court!"

"Miss Jade Miller, I'm aware that you have called Legna Mortgage, inquiring of any proposed income or estate that you should know about, and what did they say, if we may get clarity?" *the attorney queried.*

"The phone representative told me that a check written to myself had been given to Mrs. Miller," *answered Jade as her lawyer raised the exact check to their audience.*

"Mia Collins, weren't you and Pamela Cox given the check to cash at StockFarm in disguise using an expired form of identification for Jade?" *mentioned by the fifteen years of service personnel.*

Pamela Cox quickly interrupted, "I was NOT there!"

"Unfortunately for you, the elite broadband camera system on the outside captured your white Chevrolet Malibu, with license plate, VBN 642," *excluded Mrs. Stone.* "We appreciate your assertiveness, but maybe you should use that same tone when you're sitting in the doctor's office," *giving both Mr. and Mrs. Cox a wink on screen.*

"I have almost completed proving our case, your honor. It seems the crimes of our defendants may be everlasting, but this nonsense ends today!" *as a look is given to the jury from Mrs. Stone.* "A statement linked to an overseas Voodoo spiritualist was submitted containing requested services of Evil against her family, including the late husband, George Miller."

Tylor can not believe their plan has failed so terribly and began hitting his head on the McKinley Correctional wall, sensing immediate troubles came back, TENFOLD.

"Let me give you some legal advice, whether you take it or not, is up to you," *said Mrs. Stone to Mr. Cox.* "Keep your crimes to yourself next time. The mixtape you wrote gave crucial details that helped our plaintiffs instead of your fame."

Continuing her trial agreement, Mrs. Stone provided Judge William Patterson the statement from overseas, claiming Mrs. Claudia Miller confided enough to disclose that she poisoned her husband for his inheritance.

The last thing shown on screen for the court to view were pictures of Claudia's eerie attic, taken by Detective Theodore Hoffman, properly admitting her intentions of wickedness.

Judge William Patterson speaks of a short recess and when the jury has come to a verdict, the court will adjourn.

After an hour and a half, the jury is ready to give their verdict beginning with stepmother, Claudia Miller, the Killer.

The female juror stands to read,

"We the jury, have unanimously decided for the three counts of attempted murder, GUILTY."

"For two counts of her illegal crimes of forgery, GUILTY."

"For her misguided given account during an open investigation, GUILTY."

"For one count of murder, by the poisoning of George Miller, GUILTY."

Judge Patterson reads her prolonged sentence of life in prison, without parole, consecutively, detained for the next one hundred years.

Claudia falls to the floor, kicking and screaming, as the judge orders his bailiffs to take her away instantly, to start their judgment.

The jury's verdict for Pamela Cox is as follows:

"One count of forgery for signing the false marriage license, GUILTY."
"One count for being an accessory in a stolen identity scheme, GUILTY."

She is sentenced to twenty years in a federal prison, out of Louisiana.

The jury's verdict for Tylor Cox is as follows:

"Two counts of assault and battery, for the beating on Raden Smith, in using a deadly weapon, GUILTY."

"One count for being an accessory through forgery of legal government documentation, GUILTY."

"Two counts of attempted murder toward both, Jade Miller and Raden Smith, GUILTY."

He is located in McKinley Correctional Center but is transferred to a federal prison in Beaumont, Texas, for thirty-five years, without parole probation.

The last verdict of the trial goes to Mia Collins, and is as follows:

"Two counts of assault and battery for the beating of Raden Smith in using a deadly weapon, GUILTY."

"One count of stolen identity fraud, for the attempted use of personal information, at StockFarm National Bank, GUILTY."

"Two counts of attempted murder toward both, Jade Miller and Raden Smith, GUILTY."

As the pupils of her eyes grew darker, she is taken immediately to their parish jail before getting booked for the sentence of twenty-five years to life in another federal prison, out of state.

The Judge had a closing statement for both plaintiffs,

"I don't know where you two came from; however, your courage and your willingness to survive will be noticed by many."

"May God continue to bless and watch over you, as long as he permits!"

"Court is adjourned!"

A conversation needed to be held in the conference room after the trial was over, so both winning plaintiffs met with Detective Hoffman and Agent Frost. They were very excited to tell them congratulations, but their safety remained a factor until all perpetrators exceeded judgment. Jade and Raden gave each other a quick hug before departing to their separate private locations with the two US Marshalls who waited outside. The bravery showed through the work of both investigators, as they were able to sweep a path of justice starting at Chester Martinez. He would not be getting released anymore from his wide range of charges for continuous drug trafficking and their charges for ploys of murder. Kingpin Lucifer is granted a conviction of thirty-five years to life and his two partners in the legal system are without help, having problems of their own. Mia's officer cousin, Alex Collins, was found guilty of police misconduct that included the deliberate arrest of false criminals for street cred; his sentence fell on six years.

Judge Benjamin Collins had been the patriarch in their family for years; however, his act of unethical morality, committing money laundering, has prohibited him from service with an indictment of ten years incarceration. For his help regarding information for the "SMILL" case, which is from Smith and Miller, Aaron Jacobs, known as Cap, is granted immunity and released from McKinley parish jail. Naomi Jenkins apparently got charged for distributing counterfeit one-hundred-dollar bills in the community and knowingly passing around HIV; she gets a five-year sentence.

Wei Sung, better known as Tek-e, received a maximum sentence of twenty years imprisonment and fines up to $150,000 for the improper use of Social Security linked to deceased citizens. Now that God's justice has been served, District Attorney Mabel Stone had two important appointments to make, individually associated with both of her clients. Raden Smith and his lawyer went over his compensated restitution in the "SMILL" case, as the courts ordered him a payment of $1,000,000 and $15,000 in punitive damages.

Attorney Stone needed an exclusive area for Jade Miller, because certain things were not disclosed on purpose during trial, and the time called ready. Inside a quiet room at their headquarters, she was shown the original documents containing all forms of inherited detail that had never been exposed to her. Serenity Harris, the biological mother, left her entire estate to her daughter through Legna Mortgage, which Jade realized, spelled A-N-G-E-L backwards. The financial inheritance of her father, George Miller, and punitive damages from their case doubled the amount, bringing a total equivalent to $1,000,000,000, making her abundantly wealthy. Jade fell.

CHAPTER 19

THE GOLDEN ERA

The luxuries of civilization are not determined by how much currency you secure in your possession. It is insistent on the representation of true character, correlated with what or who is impairably lodged within your chest cavity. Money would no longer be an issue of restriction in the Divine Masculine and the Divine Feminine's evolution of life, though, favored notability did not faze them. What mattered could be seen through the love and light of God. Detective Hoffman spoke to Raden and Jade by phone to relay the message of change for release from their Witness Protection Program, but security would never completely halt in protection. After the trial came to a close regarding all its offenders, attention grew viral through broadcast television, the worldwide internet, and front page articles of newspapers, classified as the "SMILL" case.

No one in their local community could believe all that they endured, physically, as the two victors were missing in action. Respect for them both had become noticeable. Even though Raden was in one place and Jade another, cellular communication, brought immense joy; feelings of their encounter from eighteen years ago set fated. A blessing of fortune from God did not stop ambition. It pushed them to begin different annuities of income, producing generational wealth and entrepreneurship. Jade started writing a testimonial about what she spiritually went through while Raden took his experience in the direct start of a lucrative, statewide, eighteen-wheeled, business endeavor. With countless hours of transportation and provided employment, he gained leadership in the production of his company, showing total effort matched responsibility toward overall success.

She continued multitasking in roles of motherhood and firm self-discipline before the start of the day, waking up every morning at an earlier time to use her educational knowledge in formulating sentences and using proper grammar and resources. As life began to shift for Raden, another adversity struck him, incomparably. Back home in Louisiana, his father's health started to decline. When he arrived in town, the Smith family greeted him with open arms, stating how proud they were, but their patriarch wanted to have a serious conversation, acknowledging his change of vitality.

The following day, next to the bed, Raden sat listening to his father's request for him to find someone who truly gave love, honesty, and compassion in return. This had been so unexpected, yet, everything was heard and affirmed, where it sparked a full-blown transformation in what really mattered to him from then on. Raden decided to move forward, attracting a female's true character at heart, no longer interested in proving himself to anyone, by the status of his money or theirs. Suddenly, Mr. Smith, sad to say, passed away shortly after that. It was just before one of the most important times set for togetherness, Thanksgiving, bringing them all to a terrible grief. Jade and Raden both mysteriously started to crave the same things without either of them, even knowing so, paying attention to their words of intention during communicative transmission. Erasing their past sentimental beliefs of relationships that didn't last as lessons, they realized what mattered in importance, desperately, the want for one another and no one else. Without doing or saying much of what he is thinking, Raden speaks to his mother about meeting Jade rather soon to see her thoughts and if an approval would be given.

He tells Jade of the hope that he has for her to join him and Mrs. Smith for dinner one evening, just the three of them. She answered yes, alongside feelings of extreme nervousness, and being very flattered at the same time, to meet the woman that birthed him. Jade rumbles through her closet and dresser drawers to find the perfect outfit that is appropriately presentable for their expected occasion. At dinner, with smiles and laughter, sharing a pleasured approach, they ended their night adding the suggestion from Mrs. Smith to bring Jade over for her welcoming invite. Raden began to work on a huge project in secret, not revealing a word to anyone about what he found, irresistibly, desiring to complete.

A call comes in on Jade's phone, which is Raden, telling her to bring the kids and herself to a paid suite for a pre-vacation weekend getaway. When they reach their destination, a surprise for each child is placed on the top of both nightstands, with an enclosed note for her to call him after the kids are sleeping. After a peaceful night of enjoyment is over for them and the kids in bed by 9:00 p.m., she rings his phone, and Raden asks Jade to come across the hall to Room 513. She had no clue that he was, shockingly, there but couldn't help the thrill it gave to see his attractive face. He opens the door, greeting Jade to a peak inside his lavish, beautifully flowered suite that is purposefully arranged for two. The dining room table is prepared with champagne and two entrees, served as soft music played in the background for an intimate moment of romance. Raden stops Jade before grabbing a utensil to fall on one bended knee, confessing his love to propose a hand in marriage, making her his *first wife*.

A red box is opened, exposing a crushed-out, 10-karat white gold princess-cut ring, blinding the both of them by sight. He wasn't going to lose Jade again, with tear-flooded eyes, she said, "YES!"

They gave each other a graceful hug as their physical attraction embraced a sexual arousal, for both of them to decide, a waited night of endless passion. The excited lovers separate and Raden begins his planning for their local and exclusive marriage celebration. Everyone in their community is aware of the biggest event in town, as a fashionable event planner is hired for this sophisticated affair. Jade is invited to a location by Raden, who requested her to wear a long dress, tailor-made especially for a voluptuous frame. When they arrive together, smiling faces greet them from left and right, congratulating them on their blessed union of matrimony. Guests are able to see love in the eyes of both lovers, with the night ending around 10:00 p.m., thanking all who came and showed support.

* * *

Raden drives them away in a 2024 two-door, crescent white, Bentley Mulliner Batur headed to Las Vegas, Nevada, for their personal, privatized elope.

CHAPTER 20

ELOHIM'S PROOF

Under a full moon sky, they ride to a Vegas chapel, admiring each other with eyes of magnetized, sensational desire as love songs play softly in their background. Raden directs a bellman to bring all of their luggage to an exquisite cosmopolitan resort prearranged just for the two Divine Twin Flames. The modernized fluorescent decor interior fit a place for their harmonious ceremony, directly adjacent in structure, built convenience, and had been beautifully selected by the Divine Masculine. He opened the right door of their vehicle, escorting his Divine Feminine to walk toward the meeting chamber with him, hand in hand, for their union of wedded bliss.

A marriage officiant greets the both of them in honor and is provided the two matched bands from Raden's left suit pocket to claim their vows of commitment under God. Smiles of gratitude and love were seen on the faces of husband and wife as they presently became Mr. and Mrs. Smith with "I DO," sealing a foreordained, holy matrimony. Adding to their endless night of companionship, a Vegas chapel photographer collected some memorable portraits of representation, capturing a moment set for longevity.

The newlyweds gave each other a breathtaking kiss of temptation before heading back to their extravagant room for a night closed with intimate affection. As their door shut with a "Do Not Disturb" sign attached, Raden politely unzipped the back of Jade's gown while she began to unbutton his shirt, tasting and smelling him from the neck down.

Throughout all of this time, they waited for the chance to satisfy their yearning by touch and pleasure, savoring just enough of themselves to rest, for his ultimate surprise their following night alone. Mr. Smith comes from between the thighs of his wife to answer a room service that delivered and properly served full entrees for breakfast, offering food, beverages, and fruits plentiful for them to consume. Packing their belongings to vacate, Mrs. Smith locates two plane tickets from her husband inside of the opened luggage to Johannesburg, Gauteng, South Africa, for departure at 11:30 eastern, featuring acceptance of a honeymoon. She displayed feelings of nervousness, for this was her first time flying; however, that did not match the overall enthusiasm on her face to board a plane for an overseas trip beside the love of her life.

After a commander navigates the plane landing, airline security leads them to a chauffeured vehicle, which is suddenly instructed the drive away, bringing both to Mr. Smith's designated location. The vehicle arrived on a gray-stoned driveway that easily ascended to the front of a large contemporary-styled home, stretched with tall elongated windows and excessive indoor and outdoor lighting, and greeted by a large mass front door. When they step onto the well-constructed pavement, as endearing as one's smile could get, the Divine Masculine adds his introduction with open arms stating, "This major project had been a secret that I was keeping from you months ago," adding loudly, "WELCOME TO OUR NEW HOME, MRS. SMITH!" Filling her eyes with flowing streams, she intertwined her left arm into his right, jumping up and down, full of weight-bearing astoundment from what she had just heard.

There was beauty in every detail on the outside—from its landscape to the ground up, aiming all praise mixed with optimistic joy and overwhelming sensations of thankfulness toward such a magnificent reward from The Most High. Inside their glamorous home, a set of keys is given to Jade, as Raden takes her on a tour at night through each room space, explaining appliance features and interior design, and showing the backyard with a nature scenic view. She reaches a closed door that happens to be their spacious master bedroom. Once opened, the Divine Fem is without patience any longer, by the sight of heart balloons and rose petals trailing to their jacuzzi-sized bathtub overlooking a romantic night sea.

    A stimulation of induced passion for her masculine's touch seized control. When he enters their room, Jade begins caressing his neck with a suckling kiss of the bottom lip, breathing heavily and whispering naughty words of sexual pleasure, causing an arousal to his lower genitals in maximizable strength he'd never experienced. Jade proceeds to go down spontaneously, placing his penis in her mouth, moving the tongue in a way to entice him more, and enjoying his look of satisfaction with the taste of precum meeting the back of her throat. He removes her summer dress, without a question asked, adoring the view of the feminine's thick frame, to place his fingers inside her vagina before tearing the bottom portion of her silk panties completely off. Raden aggressively places his lover stomach down on their Alaskan king-sized bed, inhaling breaths and kissing her, softly, as each drip of candle wax off their nightstand falls onto her lower backside.

    Inserting himself inside of her, he grabs Jade's breasts, pulling a closeness between the two that intensifies their indulgence for intimacy. With heightened pressure, Raden flips her over to eat Jade's well-shaved vagina, licking the pearl tongue, explicitly, in his best delight, slurping from front to back. As she trembles with her legs in the air, sighing relief of constant pleasure, Raden continues making love to his wife in a missionary-style position, restricting her arms to move by force. Staring into the eyes, she gently kisses him, rubbing his hair, while he takes moments of sucking one nipple at a time, giving attention to both, claiming ownership of her body. Unable to control their passionate seduction, Jade climaxes in the time of her husband's erupted ejaculation, leaving sperm inside of her, releasing their first provocative round of sex and desire.

    The chemistry of their magnetic attraction lasted throughout the night, having many rounds of seduction-filled interactions, refusing to stop from physical soreness that also provided enjoyable effort. Signaling him to join her with the movement of a finger, they enter the jacuzzi for Jade to subdue Raden in a sensual motion, causing bubbles to form around them as a submissive blanket of comfort. For two people that did not believe in **true love**, until now, there sat a delicious agony that amplified, the tension of passionate freakiness, which felt surreal and illuminating toward their explanation. Visible limitless scratches were placed on their dampish bodies, from marks on Raden's upper back to Jade's inner thighs, showing evidence of their sacred love-making and inseparableness.

With a lit fireplace in the background, they rest between their satiny three-hundred-thread counted bed set, cuddling one another until the crack of dawn, body to body. Following the next day, they added furniture and colors of youthfulness to their children's rooms, preparing to get them by travel from the United States of America. Raden was just as excited as Jade to see the looks on their faces, surprising them with their very own home, making them one family under one roof. The Twin Flames put their heads together, of both taste, decorating interior and exterior designed furniture, filling their home in a suitable capacity for an attained formosity of completion. A major importance in assisting the environment and household communities has not changed. Once in South Africa, animal breeding became their popular accomplishment for a gained monetary stream of income.

They decided to hire compassionate employees who loved animals in admiration, as they did, with two choices of breeding—dogs of the elite Boerboel breed and wild lions of African Panthera descent. The mastiff dogs were placed at a site renovated in size, containing outdoor land. Equally, placement for their fierce lions sat at a separate habitat, both with consolidated security of armed personnel and twenty-four-hour monitoring. Enabling prosperity for a continuous flow of generational wealth, the Smiths' net worth tripled by billions in revenue, increasing their ability to donate funds to South African charities in need. Blueprints for stable-grounded housing properties were built from Raden's craftsmanship, purposefully, onto skirts of communities for low-income civilians.

E E Y H N V R T I G : (EVERYTHING)

They would participate in necessary spending for children of all ages by anonymously dazzling each one with their own bicycle. They gave these to children who were in attendance at a daycare or any learning facility of education. Jade begins traveling from city to city, country to country, giving her diligent voice as motivationally speaking for people of all nations, delivering speeches brought from Elohim's aggressiveness of a warned recommendation. She published her first book of completion titled "Everything," broadening a reference toward her elicit, testimonial-based miracle from His favored, supernatural experience. In her observation of the most beautiful places on Earth, Jade discovered an artwork piece, aesthetically pleasing with exquisite physical features to place inside of their home for God and His only begotten son, Jesus. The Emperor greets his wife in her return as a feeling of excitement flutters through the belly of The Empress, being later made aware that they have conceived spirit babies, a gifted set of golden twins, one boy and one girl.

On the written birthdate of their delightful children, they are startled by many entrancing sounds related to all different types of animals, surrounding their home on the outside that were sent by sky and sea from *Yours Truly*.

Unanticipatedly, this was a given universal sign of appreciation, love, and proud endearment for two counterparts of His Divine Soul Connection reaching production of a new lifecycle, a part of their fated empire provision.

For centuries on end, there have been plenty of names pertaining to God that had been sent down for our guided knowledge. ELOHIM, the plural form of El, meaning **"Strong One,"** derived from the ancient Hebrew religion.

My story of his true existence is only *One* of the many revelations.

Elohim's Proof

CONCLUSION

The Divine Twin Soulmates found their vitality in life, suitable with purposes of obedience, representation, and dignifying modesty, unremittable in companionship toward The Creator alone.

They became known for their incumbent endurance, producing strength, in acknowledgment of their own misconceptions that allotted growths of evolvement, from past to present, adversities, and afflictions. In reference to past historical calamities, each proficient wavelength of experience broadens a different attribution, with respect to a few that have limitless eternal accolades from their personal identities.

Characteristics of Prophets, such as Isa, Moses, Ibrahim, and Muhammad are carried under God's lighted favor for righteous dominations, set in courageous example, only He has sovereign to articulate as guidance for His humane society. Familiarizing teachings of persistence and durability can relatably help us all, with forgiveness to become exceptional people, in mistaken wisdom, by choice of reasonable change, incorporated with one's pursuit or destiny.

For God

You've been by my side all along and I had no clue.

*Thank You deeply, my eyes are truly
open with Your correct guidance.*

I've become a better version of myself as a woman and mother.

Making You proud is what matters most.

Please stay with me.

I love You.

www.ingramcontent.com/pod-product-compliance
Lightning Source LLC
LaVergne TN
LVHW041536070526
838199LV00046B/1687